JAMES JONES:
A Friendship

Books by Willie Morris

JAMES JONES:
A Friendship

BY WILLIE MORRIS

Doubleday & Company, Inc., Garden City, New York
1978

ISBN: 0-385-14432-6
Library of Congress Catalog Card Number 78–4709
Copyright © 1978 by Willie Morris
All Rights Reserved
Printed in the United States of America
First Edition

To Kaylie and Jamie

Author's Note

This is not a work of scholarship or of literary criticism. Rather it is an illumination of a friend, and perhaps of myself and others of us, and I hope it tells something about writing, especially about being a writer in America. Since I don't like footnotes anyway, I have identified by pages in the back of the book the sources of various quotations.

I am warmly grateful to my friend Gloria Jones for the use of many of the photographs in this book.

W.M.
Bridgehampton, Long Island
April 9, 1978

I will arise and go now, for always night and day
I hear lake water lapping with low sounds by the shore;
While I stand on the roadway, or on the pavements gray,
I hear it in the deep heart's core.

William Butler Yeats
The Lake Isle of Innisfree

JAMES JONES:
A Friendship

I .

I was sitting in Rick's, a bar on Main Street in Bridgehampton, talking with Rick and a couple of the potato farmers about baseball. From outside the big window I saw him park his car behind mine and cross the street in our direction, a pale figure in blue jeans, and a sweater, a green-and-yellow baseball cap, and the leather satchel with the strap flung over his shoulder in which he carried his cigars and a few of his knives.

He walked in and came up to me. "Your mom just died," he said. "I'm sorry."

She had gone into the hospital that week in my hometown in Mississippi. Nothing very serious, the doctors said, but I had made a reservation on the plane for the next day. She had died suddenly that morning. Some friends there had tried to telephone me at home, then called his house down the road from mine in Sagaponack.

"I been looking all over for you," he said. "The cops had it out on the radio. Come on home with me for a while. You shouldn't be alone."

Grief comes first as in a trance. Physical things stand out sharply. It is as if you are someone else, being observed from afar by yourself. Yet even in this moment, or perhaps because of it, driving through the countryside with his car following mine, I acknowledged for the first time that the two great presences in my whole life were my mother, who had just died, and this man, my friend Jim Jones; I did not know that he, too, would be dead within the month.

We drove the mile or so to his house. I had two hours before leaving for La Guardia. I telephoned the undertaker in Yazoo, and the preacher and some friends, and my son David in school in New York. I sat alone in the front room of the old farmhouse, among the hundreds of books lining the shelves. The big dog named Wade Hampton Jones lay asleep close to me, and two cats who only understood French darted here and there. I looked around at the antiques Gloria and he had brought back from their years in Paris. Outside the potato fields stretched away in a somber haze. When they moved into this house two years before I had christened it "Chateau Spud."

Jim was in the next room, writing in a notebook at the ancient wooden pulpit which they had found in the flea market and turned into a bar, then brought back to America. Near him were more shelves, dominated by the leather-bound copies of each of his ten books which he had signed for his children Kaylie and Jamie on their various birthdays—*From Here to Eternity* first, then *Some Came Running, The Pistol, The Thin Red Line,* and the others. I watched him for a while as he wrote in his notebook. He looked gaunt and tired.

He had almost died three months before. His son Jamie had come to fetch me. It was during a blizzard on a night in January. He had had another serious attack of his illness—congestive heart failure—and the men from the volunteer ambulance unit could not get the ambulance up the driveway. We had to carry him down a slippery embankment to take him to the hospital in Southampton. He had been working harder than any writer I had ever known, sometimes twelve or fourteen hours a day in the cluttered attic in this house, trying to finish the novel which had obsessed him for years, the one he considered his life's work. He called it *Whistle,* the third book in his trilogy of World War II. I had known for months he had a premonition he was fighting against time.

Now, in the next room, he turned around facing me. "Are you okay?"

I was thinking about grief, I said, how strange it is.

He emitted a characteristic sound, half sigh, half defiant growl. "There's a poem," he said. "It's one of my favorites." He went to the bookshelf and pulled out a first edition of Edna St. Vincent Millay. He thumbed the pages, then sat down and read the poem to himself.

"Do you know this one?"

I read it for a long time.

"I'll go upstairs and type it out for you. Maybe you'll want somebody to read it at your mom's funeral."

It was time to go. He came down the stairs in the chair-lift he had rigged up after his last attack to take him to and from the attic. We stood for a moment in the airy sunshine. The first touch of spring, always late to eastern Long Island, was all around us. We shook hands, in that shy, casual way old comrades do. "You know I'd go with you if I could," he said. "I have to finish *Whistle*."

On the plane to Mississippi, somewhere high over the Blue Ridge, I read the poem again before handing it to my son David.

> I am not resigned to the shutting away of loving hearts in the hard ground.
> So it is, and so it will be, for so it has been, time out of mind:
> Into the darkness they go, the wise and the lovely. Crowned
> With lilies and with laurel they go; but I am not resigned.
>
> Lovers and thinkers, into the earth with you.
> Be one with the dull, the indiscriminate dust.
> A fragment of what you felt, of what you knew,
> A formula, a phrase remains,—but the best is lost.
>
> The answers quick and keen, the honest look, the laughter, the love,—
> They are gone. They are gone to feed the roses. Elegant and curled
> Is the blossom. Fragrant is the blossom. I know. But I do not approve.
> More precious was the light in your eyes than all the roses of the world.

A month later, when Gloria and I were going through the concluding pages of *Whistle* on his worktable in the attic, two or three dozen pages before that one final page which ended

16

abruptly in the middle, there was a scribbled note in the margin: "April 15, 1977—Willie's mom died today."

Her friend Hannah Kelly played "Abide with Me" at the funeral. We buried her in the radiant Mississippi springtime in the Yazoo cemetery next to my father.

For more than thirty years she had been the organist in the Methodist church. I remember as if it were yesterday the night Miss Lizzie Hoover, the indomitable old organist, died and she had to take over. She had taught piano to four generations of Yazoo's children, on a Steinway baby grand in the parlor of our house. When I was a child I would sit in my room, on late afternoons when it began to get dark, and listen to the music from the front. I can sometimes hear her music now, after all the years, and remember the leaves falling in some smoky autumn twilight, the air crisp and the sounds of dogs barking and train whistles far away.

Once, not too long ago, she said to me, "I could hear the typewriter in your room when you were twelve years old—always scribbling on the typewriter. I knew you were going to be a writer even then. I was that way with a piano. My mother said to me when I was a little girl, 'Well, I guess you better stick with it.'" When my first book, *North Toward Home,* came out, I know some things I wrote about the town were hard on her, but she did not complain. When I was the editor of a magazine in New York, she bought more than a few subscriptions and gave them to public libraries way out in the countryside.

The town has changed remarkably little. The old houses still go by the family names of people long dead. Every house, every corner, almost every tree I associate with distant days.

17

In the schoolyards there are interracial games at recess now, and white and black children arm in arm on the boulevard we call Grand Avenue, but every facade along the way is an echo of my past. The accumulation of memory, sadness, and death among these familiar landmarks is too much—there are too many ghosts. I roam the cemetery under its elms and oaks and magnolias to see who has died since my last trip home, and touch with my hand the burial stones I knew by heart as a boy:

> *"My husband with thee departed all my hopes."*
> *"Asleep in Jesus, Blessed Thought."*
> *"God's finger touched him, and he slept."*
> *"Remembered in Life, Lamented in Death."*

The death of the last of one's parents is one of life's great divides. It brings back one's past in a rush of tenderness, guilt, regret, and old forgotten moments, tortures one with the mystery of living. What did all those moments mean? Was there any meaning to them at all? They were all dead now: my mother, my father, my grandparents, my great-aunts and -uncles. In those Christmases of childhood, the house alive with the laughter of all of my people, I was the only one there still alive. I struggled hard for the fragments of their talk, as if some secret were eluding me. I had the most acute awareness that my son and I were the last of our line.

I was there almost a month. I had to close down the house where I grew up and put it up for sale. No brothers or sisters to share that trial of finding family things in the back corners of closets—a program for my mother's piano recital in 1916, a faded photograph of my father in a baseball uniform in 1920, another of my great-grandmother holding a parasol in 1885, yellowed clippings, trinkets from high school. The movers came to take away the furniture. The last item to leave was the baby grand, which would go to the church.

I telephoned Long Island my last day there. The familiar gruff voice came on, weak and breathless now. He wasn't feeling too good, Jim said. I was driving back East in the morning, and I told him I was going to stop by the battlefield at Shiloh.

"I wish I was going too," he said. "Shiloh's one place I never got to. If you have time, check what western Tennessee looks like to see if I have the physical description right in that chapter." He paused. "Oh, shit. You had to close down your house, didn't you?"

The moment came that I stood alone in the empty house. Did I know then how it would grow to haunt my dreams and nightmares? In the gloom of it that day I strained to hear the music again, my father's footsteps on the porch, the echoes of boys playing basketball in the back yard, the barks and whines of Tony, Sam, Jimbo, Sonny, Duke, and Old Skip. I locked the front door and did not look behind me.

Late the next night, from the motel in the Pickwick Dam State Park just across the Mississippi line in Tennessee and only a few miles down the road from Shiloh, I telephoned again. Gloria had taken him that afternoon to the hospital. He was very sick. "I think it's time for you to get on back," she said.

Just west of Nashville I hit the big expressways, a world to themselves, keeping the speedometer precisely at seventy. The great landmarks of America drifted past: Knoxville and the Smokies, the mountain villages of Bristol and Abingdon, the

Shenandoah Valley, the mists of the Blue Ridge and the Massanutten, Lexington and Winchester and Harpers Ferry, where Jim and I had brought our sons only a year before, on into Pennsylvania and New Jersey.

It seems I am forever traveling out of the South and into the North, the magnetic points on the compass of my existence, and this was now to me, in retrospect, one of the cataclysmic journeys of my life. Caught there in the serenity of a fast-moving car, using the big diesels to run interference, stopping only for coffee or gas or to sleep or to empty my bladder, I felt the South recede as an element of nature recedes. Ever since my boyhood, driving through the South had never failed to suffuse me with a bittersweet sadness, the sadness of love and belonging, and now something there had ended for me, something irretrievably lost in the land I knew in my heart, some connecting vein with one's own mortality. In the trunk of the car, sealed in a cardboard box, was the family silver, which I had not entrusted to the movers—the same family silver which my great-grandmother had hidden from the Northern troops when they took the town in 1863. On these interminable stretches of freeway, in a drive I managed to make in slightly more than two days, I thought of my friend who lay dying in a hospital out at the easternmost littoral of America. His fate, and the solitary farewell in Mississippi, became enmeshed for me on this drive, one of those junctures which, once passed, becomes symbolic almost, and makes a man ask: What now?

2.

I had met him for the first time about ten years before, at a party for him and Gloria in New York City at Jean and William vandenHeuval's apartment on Central Park West, one of the places where people met in those days.

I knew much about him from a distance. I had read almost everything he had written, and believed *From Here to Eternity*, *The Thin Red Line*, and *Some Came Running* three of the finest novels in American literature. When I first read *From Here to Eternity* in college, I was stunned by its power. It was one of those American novels which in youth touches one with a sense of discovery. It evoked for me the timely yet timeless quality of a place and an era, suspended there for an instant before that morning in December. The scene at Schofield Barracks when Private Robert E. Lee Prewitt sounds taps was as memorable to me in those days as young Ike McCaslin's confrontation with the bear in Faulkner's novella (the setting of which, as I plotted it out geographically then, was the delta forests of my own home county), as Twain's storm on the Mississippi in *Huck Finn,* or as Wolfe's pages on the death of Gant in *Of Time and the River.* Other passages in *Some Came Running, The Pistol,* and *The Thin Red Line* affected me deeply, as they did so many others. I knew then, long before I met him, that the Army was, in truth, his Yoknapatawpha County; like Faulkner, he could not get away from it even when he wanted to. From book to book the names changed, but the characters remained the same, with cryptic keys to their similarity—so that, for instance, Sergeant Warden in *From Here to Eternity* became Sergeant Welsh in *The Thin Red Line* (and, subsequently, Sergeant Winch in *Whistle*), and in the same way, Stark-Storm-Strange and Prewitt-Witt-Prell. As I grew older I recognized that by his hardearned craftsmanship he had enlarged the limits of the language in America as perhaps no other writer of his time had done. As Irwin Shaw later wrote, his work "came from a group of men who spoke plainly, without euphemisms, using words about death and sex and cowardice and chicanery and despair that before Jones had rarely been on the printed page in this country. From the stink of the battlefield and the barracks came a bracing, clear wind of truth. To use a military term, he walked point for his company." Later I felt that the more hostile of the critics seemed to be assessing an altogether different writer from the one I admired, as if he had committed that most unpardonable of literary crimes—great success too early.

I had read articles about him in *Life* and *Esquire* and other magazines. I knew he had grown up in Robinson, Illinois, the son of a father who killed himself and a mother he hated—a tortured and lonely childhood. I knew he had made a lot of money and owned a house on the Île St.-Louis where the Americans in Paris congregated, with plenty of poker games and hard drinking. And barroom fights with cracked ribs and broken teeth to show for them, and cocktails on Boulevard St. Michel or the older expatriate cafes of Montparnasse at twilight, and afternoons at the track. Despite four years of Oxford and numerous trips to the Continent, I was never part of that world, but I sometimes wished I had been—it sounded romantic, part of the writing life. I had heard about the trips to the Mediterranean, weekends in Deauville, summers in Greece, skin diving in the Caribbean. I knew about his years in a trailer camp in Illinois when he was writing under the patronage of Lowney Handy. I knew also, from mutual friends such as Rose and William Styron and Irwin Shaw, that he was beloved by many people, and that he had one of America's most beautiful, funny, lovable, and no-holds-barred wives.

I did not know then, but he told me later, of the time he was discharged from the Army after months in hospitals, with a damaged ankle and not all that good in the head, when he went to the mountains around Asheville, North Carolina, because he had been absorbed by Thomas Wolfe, and rented a cabin from a farmer and drank a lot of corn whiskey in solitude and ate new potatoes and green corn and green beans to try and get over the war. The combat had been bad enough, but he was all alone taking a shit behind a rock by a ravine one day when a half-starved Japanese soldier came out at him from the jungle, and after a struggle he had to kill him with a knife, and then he found the family photographs in the dead man's wallet; for a time he refused to fight again, and they put him in the stockade and busted him to private. Nor did I know that he came to New York City after Carolina and wrote a novel, then went to the Scribner's office and de-

talked reminded me a little of my father, who was a small-town boy from western Tennessee, but with the profanity added.

"Holy shit, it's hot," he said. He proceeded to take off his coat and roll up his sleeves. I did likewise. We were standing near the bar, and he left momentarily to talk with some new arrivals. The bartender had vanished into the kitchen. Suddenly Ted Kennedy came up to me and extended his glass. "Another scotch and soda, please," he said. This swift motion took me by surprise. I made the drink and handed it to him. It took me a few seconds to realize he had mistaken me for the bartender. From a distance I noticed that this scene had not been lost on Jim Jones. He was laughing so hard he put his hand against the wall for support. Soon Kennedy came up to me again: "What were *you* doing there? Let me fix *you* a drink." When he left Jim walked over to me and said, "I told him you ain't the bartender, you're the fuckin' editor in chief of *Harper's Magazine*."

Why did we become like brothers? He was almost fifteen years older than I. The morning he stood huddled against the dayroom wall of Schofield Barracks clutching a half-pint of milk and saw the two lines of holes that kept popping up on the asphalt and then the pilot with the red suns on his plane's wings flying so low that the pilot waved at him and grinned, I was hiding in the quilts of my bed crying out of fear that the Japs would attack Yazoo County next. Among the countless people you meet in a lifetime—in a classroom as a child, on a plane, in a bar, through friends—is it possible when you first begin talking with them to foresee that someday they might be among the very few of all human beings, or perhaps the only one of all of them, to share something immeasurably close and enduring? It was not coincidental that our friendship began and deepened at that point in his life when he had about decided to come on home, and that eventually, in 1974, he and Gloria and their children ended up down the way in Sagaponack.

I was to learn over the years that beneath the rough exterior was a profoundly cultured and sophisticated man, a student of literature, history, art, and music. He loved a good time more than most, and had the craziest, most shit-eating laugh. He had always had, too, an almost religious dedication to his work. Up until two days before he died he would be talking into a tape recorder about his novel. Even with the final collapse of his body he was the sanest man I ever knew. He was, in the truest and best sense, an old-fashioned man. He and his work were all of a piece; I never knew anyone who was more like his own writing, so attuned to the deep, informing spirit of it. He could not stand fraud, or phoniness, or meanness, and often he would respond to the remark of some pompous or devious ass with the enlisted man's contemptuous "Sir?" His lowest tolerance was for gratuitous cruelty, in a person, in a piece of writing. Yet—and I could recount two dozen instances to illuminate it—he had an almost heroic patience and kindness for all sorts of harmless fools and charlatans. He knew a great deal about the vagaries of the human head, and they bemused him. "Oh, it's just human beings trying to work things out despite themselves," he might say of something that had happened—"not doing too good, but trying." He knew firsthand the terrible price exacted for civilization. As with his character Mast in *The Pistol*, he sometimes had "an intense, gloomy sense of tragedy and sorrow, and a sad, resigned melancholy." Yet he loved life, and was gentle in it, because he knew so much about death. One of the many ironies about him was that he knew from his own experience so much

became claustrophobic for me, a gripping claustrophobia which filled me with horror. Taxicab rides through the steam coming out of the sewers chilled me to the bone. The street scenes which intrigued so many suffused me with unease. The shortness of memory—the absence of the quality of remembrance, of the passing of time as associated with people and places—caused me to suffer. The savagery of the intellectual discourse in those Vietnam years became unbearable to me, and for a while I tried not to say anything harsh about anybody. That, I suppose, was my final capitulation. "Ideological words have a way of wearing thin," Walker Percy of Mississippi wrote, "and then, having lost their meanings, being used like switchblades against the enemy of the moment." I had found immense gratification in editing a good, serious magazine, one that had meaning to the times, and working with a number of the great writers of our day—writers whose work, by God, was going to last—several of whom would become close and honored friends. Sweeping changes were taking place in American society—the women's movement, the integration of the black people into the fabric of the South and the emergence of that region from its traditional role as the denigrated loser and crucible of the nation's guilt, the uses of the language. (Norman Mailer's *On the Steps of the Pentagon*, taking up the entire issue of a month in 1968, had had a major effect on the country. Most of the hundreds of subscription cancellations were not over the anti-Vietnam position, but over the four-letter words.) Our magazine was in the very center of all these things, abetting them in most cases, but I think dealing with them in a spirit of civility, and holding to light the abrasive excesses. I felt strongly, as Arthur Schlesinger, Jr., wrote of those days, "the fragility of the membranes of civilization, stretched so thin over a nation so

28

disparate in its composition, so tense in its interior relationships, so cunningly enmeshed in its underground fears and antagonisms." I remember well the June afternoon when Schlesinger delivered the commencement address to the graduates of City University in Bryant Park as Bobby Kennedy lay dying in Los Angeles; after the ceremonies I followed Schlesinger to his offices across the street and we shared a bottle of scotch and watched the fading afternoon from the window overlooking the park, and he asked me in his sorrow: "What's happening to our country?"

But there comes a time, in the words of a Woody Guthrie song of the 1960s, when a man feels deep down somewhere that he's "laid around, and stayed around, this old town too long." I left it—I had only just turned thirty-six—and tried to get down to my own work. Jim Jones, too, as with many writers, felt he had served his years in the city and seldom went in any more unless he had to—"I wouldn't live there now unless incarcerated," he said—and when he did he usually conducted his business as quickly as possible, then went to P. J. Clarke's and sat at a table in the back room and talked with the old friends who drifted through.

For a while I was rather self-righteous about fraudulence and the petty conceits. The way people dropped you was a good lesson to learn. Yet for a time I found myself missing some of the perquisites of a position of relatively high station, not to mention the deferences and minor attentions. Jim was not much for the ceremonial trimmings. The honesty and courage and unadorned values of the man were tempered, yet enhanced, by his simplicity. He was a man of deep moral principle, of an ultimate bedrock integrity, a declaration I would not make lightly. Nor do I believe it silly for me to say that he set an example for me, as he did for a lot of people.

We shared a love for literature, America, the South, sitting around and telling stories—shared, too, a distrust of ideologues. He was a prop, a pillar. He knew about character because he had character.

On my long journey from the South, as the springtime crept northward up the continent, I dwelled on those things I had grown to know of Jim—the days in the infantry and in hospitals, the apprenticeship in writing, the overnight success, the years in Paris, the exile which was not really exile, the coming home:

3.

Robinson, Illinois, is a small town in the Wabash River Valley, not too far from the Indiana line. "Down south in Illinois," he said, "—Copperhead country." He was born there on November 6, 1921. His great-grandmother was a full Cherokee, and his grandfather was the sheriff and later a lawyer and wrote a book called *The Trials of Christ and Were They Legal?* The grandfather had four sons. "For some reason all of them turned out weak, mean, not very strong," Jim would say. All of them had college educations, and when the Depression came all of them lost the money they had inherited from their father, who had become rich after oil was discovered on his farm. He grew up in a substantial Victorian house surrounded by big trees, but it was not happy inside. His mother, Ada, came from Iowa and went to the University of Chicago. She was a Christian Scientist and suffered from congestive heart failure. He found her domineering, cruel, and deceitful; he called her a "dwarf" and said she had "the mind of a mole." His father, Ramon, was a dentist and the town drunk. There was affection between the father and son. Later the son would write a short story called "Just Like the Girl," the most autobiographical story he ever wrote, he said, about a mother in a Midwestern town persuading her young son to hide in the back of his father's car to spy for her on his carousing. He had an older brother, Jeff, who went to Northwestern before the money ran out, and a sister, Mary Ann, four years younger than he, who died of a brain tumor in 1956 and to whom he would write a moving dedication to *Some Came Running*.

He was an excellent student and read a lot—the family had an extensive library in the classics—but he did not go to college because the family was broke. There was a war coming anyway. In 1939 his father advised him to join the Army and to request service in the Pacific, because all the fighting, he said, would be in Europe. "I was in a unique position," the son later wrote, "in that I was born into the upper classes (such as they were in my small town), and for personal and economic reasons of my own enlisted in the old Regular Army; and then, since then, have moved back in among the upper classes by reason of a certain success as a writer. But even back then I was always confused by the slippage and discrepancy between these two systems of ideals." While he was in Hawaii his mother died; a year later his father killed himself with a pistol, a harrowing thing; the first bullet wounded him badly but did not kill him. He managed to shoot himself a second time in the head.

He was sent to Schofield Barracks at the age of eighteen in

1939 as a private in the old Hawaii Division, its insignia the green poi leaf. He started reading books diligently. He learned to know every shelf in the post library. "It was there," he later remembered, "that I first picked up Thomas Wolfe's *Look Homeward, Angel* and heard some 'mystic' call telling me I was a writer." Wolfe awakened him to the possibilities of the language as he did a whole generation of young American men. He found similarities between his family in Illinois and Wolfe's Gants. "Wolfe's home life seemed so similar to my own and his feeling about himself so similar to mine about myself," he would recall to A. Scott Berg, "that I realized I had been a writer all my life without knowing it or having written. Once I made up my mind, it seemed inevitable, something fate had directed ever since my birth." Later he started reading Faulkner, Steinbeck, Hemingway, and Fitzgerald, and managed to take two or three English courses at the university in Manoa Valley in his free time.

He was on the boxing team, fighting as a lightweight. And sometimes he got into trouble in the bars and fleshpots along Hotel Street in Honolulu, places which would become the Black Cat, the Blue Anchor, and the whorehouse he would call the New Congress Hotel, Alma's place. In his Army career he rose to the rank of sergeant, and would be busted twice to private. He never ended up in Schofield's notorious stockade, but he was friends with the kind of soldiers who did. The compulsion in a young person to remember things and to wish to write about them someday is an inexplicable chemistry. He kept a notebook in his pocket. One knows he knew a great deal about the stockade and the stone quarry and the framed bungalows which were the officers' quarters at Schofield and the golf course where Prewitt died trying to rejoin the company at Hanuama Bay. He knew, too, how much the dog soldier's life and the blues were of a piece:

> Get paid on Monday
> Not a dog soldier no more
> They gimme all that money
> So much my pockets is sore
> More dough than I can use
> Reenlistment Blues . . .
> Ain't no time to lose.
> Reenlistment Blues.

Schofield Barracks was probably the U. S. Army's most beautiful post, with "long stretches of green lush lawn, and short palms and tall palms and spreading hardwoods thrusting up here and there out of its rolling expanses." Its backdrop was Kole Kole Pass to the west, which he always thought of as The Pregnant Woman, and she moved him—"Mt. Kaala the highest point was her belly, Waianae Peak her knees, Peacock Flats her shins, and the cut at the pass made her long flowing hair, dropping straight from a jutting face-shaped ridge." His company marched in formation out Kole Kole Road, past the baseball diamond to the empty field beyond for close-order drill, and past the golf course for squad and platoon small-unit tactics. Then the ranges in the hills for mortar, rifle, and artillery. Twice he marched up Kole Kole alone, with a full field pack and a non-com as escort over an argument he had had with the company commander, just as Prewitt would do. In later life to friends he would call all this "Hono-Fuckin'-Lulu," in complicated affection.

Not long before the sneak attack the 25th "Tropical Lightning" Infantry Division replaced the Hawaii Division and would bear the shoulder patch of the poi head with a streak of lightning running vertically through it. It would be the division of Jim Jones and Prewitt and Maggio and Warden and Chief Choate and Stark and Captain Dynamite Holmes, and it would go through Guadalcanal and New Georgia and the liberation of the Philippines all the way to the occupation of mainland Japan, although his own fighting days would end on Guadalcanal. More than thirty years later, in the attic where he worked, he kept a photograph of his company—Company F—taken in November 1941 in D Quad of Schofield, a haunting picture, and there he is on the second row looking unexpectedly young and innocent, as if he is waiting for something to happen, and only the slightest imaginative leap will embrace those men as the full cast of the novel which would someday make them more real than reality. Later he would ink in "KIA" and "WIA" and "Tr" (for transferred) on the chests of many of the men in the photograph. "I kept tabs," he said.

On the morning of December 7, after the attack started, he went to the guard orderly desk outside the colonel's office of the old 27th Regiment quadrangle to carry messages for distraught officers, wearing an issue pistol he was later able to make off with as Private Mast did in *The Pistol*. In mid-afternoon of that day his company, along with hundreds of others, pulled out of Schofield for their defensive beach positions. A Japanese land invasion was expected. As they passed Pearl Harbor they could see the rising columns of smoke for miles around.

I shall never forget the sight as we passed over the lip of the central plateau and began the long drop down to Pearl City. Down toward the towering smoke columns as far as the eye could see, the long line of army trucks . . . wound serpentlike up and down the draws of red dirt through the green of cane and pineapple. Machine guns were mounted on the cab roofs of every truck possible. I remember thinking with a sense of the profoundest awe that none of our lives would ever be the same, that a social, even a cultural watershed had been crossed which we could never go back over, and I wondered how many of us would survive to see the end results. I wondered if I would. I had just turned twenty the month before.

In the following months they built defenses and guarded the Oahu beaches with their .30-caliber water-cooled machine guns; one gets a feeling for these lonely, windswept days following the attack in *The Pistol*. He rolled barbed wire along the beach, and the company commander got permission to put up a gate of concertina so they could swim. He also helped construct several pillboxes at the remote Makapuu Head. They used their bare hands and gasoline-driven jackhammers that would not shut off like pneumatic drills when you moved them. They dug five pillboxes in the virgin rock there, floored and roofed them and apertured them with concrete, then in shifts they stared through the apertures, waiting for the Japanese. More than three decades later, in 1973, he went back to Hawaii on a touching personal odyssey; he went out alone to this acutely desolate terrain looking for these pillboxes:

> My feet started carrying me up the complex of faded paths as surely as though they knew the way before my eyes did.

They were all there. All five of them. Somebody at some point had bricked the apertures shut, but most of them had been broken open. The hewn-rock stairs down into two of them had been blocked by rubble and trash, but by shouldering the steel doors of the other three I could get into those. I stood in each of them a long time, looking out and remembering times when late at night I had sat behind machine-guns in all of them, staring out into the dark toward Rabbit Island and the beach that faced it.

When I came up out of the last one and started back down, I looked down and automatically placed my foot on a natural step in the rock that we had always used to climb in or out. It was still there, unchanged, uneroded, unchipped. And my foot still knew where it was. I stood staring down at it for several seconds, shocked, and when I looked back up and looked down the hill at the tourists and the clustered cars, it was as if I were back there in 1942, when the overlook was empty, peering forward into an unforeseeable future when it would be open and crowded with sightseers, as it was now. The only thing that was different was that I was alone, that there was nobody with me.

Foolishly, I began taking pictures. As if pictures could capture what was happening to me. In a way I felt I was bearing witness—bearing the witness I had come back to Hawaii to authenticate. But just exactly what it was—except a thumbing of my nose at time—I didn't know.

He would remember an unexpected windfall out there on the beaches. A half-Hawaiian gentleman drove up in a pickup truck with four wahines in the back. The four girls went into one of the pillboxes and, with the sergeant and the lieutenant looking the other way, took care of thirty-seven of them in just forty-five minutes. The charge was ten dollars a man and everybody was happy with the price.

Company F did not get passes into town for six months. With his first pass, he walked into the bar of the Waikiki Tavern near the Moana Hotel and ran into three sailors off the carrier *Yorktown,* in Pearl for repairs to bomb damage after the Battle of the Coral Sea. They were putting away immense amounts of booze—"might not get another chance," one of them said—and they began telling him about the desperate battle they had just been through.

> "Listen, we better not be telling him all this," one of the sailors said anxiously.
> "Aw, shit," the petty officer snarled. "Look at him. You think he's some Jap spy?"
> "What about that bartender?" the sailor said.
> "Fuck it," the petty officer said. "I've known that bartender for ten years."

He stayed with the three sailors through most of the day, until they were so drunk they could hardly stand up.

> With their sun-blackened faces and hollow haunted eyes, they were men who had already passed into a realm I had never seen, and didn't particularly want to see. As the petty officer said, factually, it wasn't the going there the one time, but the going back again and again, that finally got to you.

The rumors were that the 25th would ship out to Australia. But near the end of August 1942, he was in one of three convoys which left Honolulu for Guadalcanal, where the exhausted 1st Marines had been involved in the first real American offensive and some of the most vicious fighting of the entire war. The division unloaded into landing boats off Guadalcanal and landed on the open beaches.

> When you are not straining and gasping to save your life, the act of doing so can seem adventurous and exciting from a distance. The greater the distance the greater the adventure.
>
> But, God help me, it was beautiful. I remember exactly the way it looked the day we came up on deck to go ashore: the delicious sparkling tropic sea, the long beautiful beach, the minute palms of the copra plantation waving in the sea breeze, the dark green band of jungle, and the dun mass and power of the mountains rising behind it to rocky peaks . . . From the mountain slopes in mid-afternoon with the sun at your back you could look back down to the beach and off across the straits to Florida Island and one of the most beautiful views of tropic scenery on the planet. None of it looked like the pestilential hellhole that it was.

There was an air raid that day they got there, Japanese planes trying to bomb their transport ships. Those of them already on shore stood near some trees and watched, he remembered, as if it were a football game or a movie. Whenever a Jap plane was hit in the sky, the Marine and Army veterans would let out a cheer, and soon the new arrivals were doing it with them. A loaded barge took a hit and seemed to disappear. It seemed strange and calloused, he thought, to be watching and cheering when men were dying.

Later, after our first time up on the line, we would sit in our bivouac on the hills above Henderson Field and watch the pyrotechnic display of a naval night battle off Savo Island with the same insouciance, and not feel callous at all. They took their chances and we took our chances.

Before the later battles of "massed armadas, masses of newer equipment, and massed units of men in division and corps strength," there was a primitiveness to the fighting on Guadalcanal. Small platoon and company units still carried importance. "There was," he wrote later, "an air of adventure and sense of individual exploit about it." Out of all this, of course, would come, in 1962, the great combat novel of American literature, *The Thin Red Line*.

The most horrible thing about being green was that the new soldier "didn't know what to look for or listen for, or smell for."

No amount of training behind his own lines could teach him what it was like to move out beyond them where there might be enemy. Where, eventually, there was sure to be enemy. But where? How did he look for them? What did he listen for? Those men seriously meant to kill him. Beyond the lines, a strange still breathlessness seemed to come down and settle on things: trees, roads, grass. Handling his fear was another problem. Learning to live with it, and to go ahead in spite of it, took practice and a certain overlay of bitter panache it took time to acquire. There were damned few fearless men. I knew, I think, two personally. But they were both crazy, almost certifiably so. That made them good soldiers . . .

So there he stood—our once green, now obscene infantryman or tanker. Filthy, grimy, bearded, greasy with his own body oils (body oils aided by a thin film of dirt could make a uniform nearly completely waterproof, if it was worn long enough), dedicated to his own survival if at all possible, and willing to make it as costly as he could if it wasn't possible . . . He was about the foulest-mouthed individual who ever existed on earth. Every other word was fucking this or fucking that. And internally, his soul was about as foul and cynical as his mouth . . . He had pared his dreams and ambitions down to no more than relief and a few days away from the line, and a bottle of booze, a woman, and a bath.

After the fighting came, he reached "the individual soldier's final full acceptance of the fact that his name is already written down in the rolls of the already dead."

Every combat soldier . . . must, I think, be led inexorably to that awareness. He must make a compact with himself or with Fate that he is lost. Only then can he function as he ought to function, under fire. He knows and accepts beforehand that he's dead, although he may still be walking around for a while.

In a costly three-day fight for a group of hills called The Galloping Horse, he was hit in the head by a fragment from a random mortar shell and spent some time in the hospital before returning up the line. He arrived at the regimental aid station with his head all covered with blood, feeling dizzy and a little hysterical, and ran into their old regimental surgeon, a

light colonel, cutting strips of flesh out of a wound in the back
of a boy sitting there on a table. The doctor looked up from
his work and saw the new arrival.

"Hello, Jonesie," the doctor said casually. "Getting more
material for that book of yours you're gonna write?"

"More than I want, Doc," he replied, laughing—he remembered—very crazily.

Of all the countless dead he saw in those weeks—the dead
lying mutilated in rows, or individual corpses blending into
the stench and lushness of the jungle—he would somehow
remember one boy most of all. It happened to be the day that
he was hit by the mortar fragment.

> I had had to cross a grassy little gulch, and had to
> climb a long steep hillside through sparse jungle
> trees. I was being fired at by snipers—puffs of dirt
> kept popping up around me from time to time—but
> I couldn't climb any faster. Halfway up the hill I
> came upon a stretcher with a dead boy in it that had
> been abandoned. It lay among some rocks, tilted a
> little, just the way it had been dropped. He had obvi-
> ously been hit a second time, in the head, and left by
> the stretcher bearers, probably under fire themselves
> . . . Blood had run out of him from somewhere until
> it nearly filled the depression his hips made in the
> stretcher. And that has always stayed with me. It
> didn't seem a body could hold enough blood to do
> that. His hips were awash in it and it almost covered
> his belt and belt buckle. And somehow, though he
> was lying on his back, head uphill, blood had run or
> splashed from his head so that there were pools of it
> filling both his eye sockets . . . He looked so pathetic
> lying there, one hand dangling outside the stretcher,

that I wanted to cry for him. But I was gasping too hard for breath, and was too angry to cry for anybody.

"Hours after terror, and the hot dry mouth of fear, men back out of a fight or back off the line could begin to wrinkle their eyes a little and smile again." When they were not fighting they were getting drunk, on a vile concoction they fermented themselves from canned fruit and called "swipe." One night a tough little Southerner in his unit told them he had promised himself and God in the last firefight that if he came out of it in one piece he would crawl across the ground and bay like a dog at the moon, and after several drinks of swipe "he proceeded to get down in his clean uniform in the mud and wriggle along through it like a man hunting a hole under fire, throwing back his head and stretching his neck and baying like a hound at the big full tropical moon under the coco palms." They stood there insanely drunk and cheered him on, until finally an officer sent a sentry over to tell them to stop the racket. Or they would look at the pinups of Paulette Goddard, Jane Russell, Ann Sheridan, Barbara Stanwyck, and Betty Grable in the Army papers. "They were innocent and ughsville, unattractive with their bare knees, half-thighs and carefully hidden breasts; to look at them you would not think the women of those days ever had crotches and tits, or even armpits." Or they would laugh a lot at such people as the man who came down with the clap in that womanless jungle campaign, or the soldier in the company's forward platoon who got an erection during a halfhearted Japanese attack, or the infantryman who refused to walk any more. This latter individual had been given a month in the stockade for refusing to walk, and when he came out he became a jeep driver. He would not even walk to the latrine. "When he had to go, he would come out of his shelter, drive the jeep fifty yards to the latrine, and hop out. When he had finished his crap, he would drive the jeep back to the CP. He had made his separate peace."

Sometimes, when they were down the line but about to go into combat again, a loudspeaker would blare out to them some of the popular tunes of the day. He would remember one song in particular that they played, and later think how unfair and cruel it was, to play this to those boys in such moments:

> I'll be seeing you,
> In every lovely summer's day,
> In everything that's bright and gay,
> I'll always think of you that way,
> I'll see you in the morning's sun
> Or when the day is through,
> I'll be looking at the moon
> But I'll be seeing you.

In March 1943 after they had prosecuted the final bloody offensive on the 'Canal and pushed the Japanese back to Tassafaronga, the 25th prepared to move up to New Georgia. He had had a bad ankle since long before Pearl Harbor. He would tape it up before going out on maneuvers or up on the line. One day, walking through the bivouac with his old first sergeant, he turned the ankle again and fell in the mud. "You're crazy," the sergeant said. "Didn't you show that leg to them up at division?"

> He had presented me with a serious moral problem. I talked it over with a few of my buddies, and

with a few of the other non-coms in the company. All of them urged me to go up to division medical with it. They would certainly go up with it if they had it, if they were me and maybe it could get them out of there . . . "But what about the company?" I asked the mess sergeant, and supply sergeant, and a couple of the field sergeants.

"Are you kidding?" the supply sergeant said. "I'd be out of here like a shot."

The surgeon at division examined the ankle and told him he had no business in the infantry. He shipped him out to the hospital at Efate in the New Hebrides. The young head surgeon at Efate operated the day after he got there. Ten days later he was sent to New Zealand on another hospital ship. Three weeks after that he left on another for the States.

When we passed under the great misty pink apparition of the Golden Gate Bridge, I stood on the upper decks on my crutches and watched grizzled tough old master sergeants and chief petty officers break down and cry. I had been away three and a half years.

He was among the first large waves of wounded shipped back from the Pacific to California, and then by hospital train to various points in the States. In what, many years later, would become the novel *Whistle*, there are strong autobiographical echoes in the months he spent in the Kennedy General Hospital in Memphis, which he would fictionalize as Luxor, and later when he was on Limited Duty at Camp Campbell in Kentucky. He was still reading extensively, and putting notes down on paper, a practice he had continued on

Guadalcanal. He had brought some of these notes back with him, and later could hardly read them, they were so caked with mud. There was one small notebook which he kept in those days in Memphis, with a long list of girls and their telephone numbers, and a strange muted comment on one of its pages: "The Army is killing the creativity in me." Whatever mystery it is that gets a man there, he was twenty-two years old and a writer.

The hospital in Memphis had a "grim and iron-clad mood." The men did not laugh very much about their wounds, the way they did in *The Saturday Evening Post*. They knew and talked of the less fortunate ones who were blind, or paralyzed, or awaiting amputations. There were two full wards of foot and leg amputations alone from frozen feet in the Attu invasion in the Aleutians, "where some forgetful planner had sent the troops in in leather boots." Many of the less serious cases, too, lived with the knowledge that as "retreads" they would eventually be reassigned to new units and sent back to combat in Europe, just as Sergeant Strange would be in *Whistle*.

After a time the walking wounded would get passes from the hospital to go into Memphis. Everything rankled them: the unrealistic war movies which all seemed to have rules like football games, the home-front confidence. It was a different America altogether from the one so many of them had left before the war. There was an unexpected affluence everywhere. Everyone had a cynical, knowing grin. Everyone seemed to be getting rich. In the summer of that year—1943—he was riding on a street bus and heard one plant worker say to another: "If this son-of-a-bitching fucking war only lasts two more years, I'll have it made for life." And he could not get angry at the man. He felt he understood him—the man was just another worker who remembered the Depression. Some of the over-

seas men went back on crowded buses or trains to their home-
towns on furlough, and often got drunk and in trouble because they could not talk with anyone, most of all their
families. And they would return to the hospital glad to be
once again among those who had lived through the same
things they had. The future author knew about Greyhound
rides home during these war years, and would write of one
such journey in *Whistle:*

> The ride itself was a long half-waking nightmare
> of heavy-smelling bodies, paper-wrapped bologna
> sandwiches, swollen feet, toilet stops, beers, half
> pints of whiskey, oncoming headlights flashing uneas-
> ily over the sleeping faces in the darkened interior.

When they were out on passes, they frequented the Peabody Hotel on Union Street (right down the way from the
Gayosa, where Nathan Bedford Forrest had astounded the
Northern officers during the occupation of Memphis by riding
his horse through the lobby)—a place I myself remember
well from my trips to Memphis when I was growing up 150
miles away down in Yazoo City, Mississippi.

> The great influx of servicemen had taken it over
> from the local gentry, and at just about any time of
> day or night there were always between half-a-dozen
> and a dozen wide-open drinking parties going in the
> rooms and suites, where it was easy to get invited
> simply by walking down the corridors on the various
> floors until you heard the noise.
> Money was not much of a problem. Nor were
> women. There was always plenty of booze from
> somebody, and there were also unattached women at

the hotel floor parties. You could always go up to the Starlight Roof and find yourself a nice girl and dance with her awhile and bring her down. Everybody screwed. Sometimes, it did not even matter if there were other people in the room or not at the swirling kaleidoscopic parties. Couples would ensconce themselves in the bathrooms of the suites and lock the door.

When they could get away from the hospital, it was to the parties in the Peabody that the wounded members from the old company—Winch, Prell, Strange, Landers—would come in *Whistle*.

As with many of the overseas men, he got eleven months' back pay at a corporal's rate. With this, and an allotment he had been sending home to a bank for quite a few years to go to college on when he got out of the Army, he had more than four thousand dollars. He and two others from the hospital rented a suite in the Peabody at full rates for two months. When they were unable to leave the hospital, they gave the keys to someone else. Their suite became one of the big party spots. Most of the girls who flocked to their suite were defense plant workers from small towns in the middle South who had migrated to Memphis for the jobs and the excitement.

I often shuddered to think what their trembling fingers might do next day to some piece of armament destined for some poor dogface in the mud of Italy or the Pacific. But in a mass war as mass as our war was a mass, one man couldn't take account of everything. Besides, if they were cautioned to go home and sober up and get some sleep before going to work at the plant, they would only leave us and go down the hall to the next suite's party on the floor below. And we would be out a girl, and the poor Government Issue in Italy would be no better off.

He knew a fellow in the hospital who had had a hand nearly blown off in the Pacific from a faulty grenade with a short fuse.

> When they finally let him out on pass, I went out with him drinking a couple of times. He certainly had a way with women. He was a cheerful, rapacious, malevolent type of a guy, and claimed that because of what the bad grenade had done to his hand, it was his project to screw every riveter, welder, lathe-operator, and fuse-cutter that he could get his one good hand on for the rest of the War. That was to be his revenge. The little I saw of him, it appeared he might realize his ambition.

On the dance roof of the Peabody, the band would end every evening by playing the national anthem. The wounded overseas men from Kennedy General often would not stand up while it was being played; they felt they had done enough. One night he got into a bloody fistfight with a couple of sailors who challenged him to pay more respect to *The Star-Spangled Banner*. The fight raged out into the corridor and eventually into an elevator, and thirty-five years later this would become one of the most powerful scenes in *Whistle*.

A "wrenching social upheaval and realignment," he noted later of these years, "accounted for an almost total breakdown of the moral standard of prewar U.S. living." While he was based in the Memphis hospital, he spent a brief furlough with his older brother Jeff in Miami Beach.

Platoons and companies of young-looking OCS cadets marched through the golf courses and ritzy shopping areas shouting out old army rhymes to the command "Count off!" In marching rhymes and at the top of their lungs they sang songs like "I've Been Working on the Railroad" and "Roll a Silver Dollar" and "For Me and My Gal." The government had taken over most of the hotels along the beach, for the use of depleted and nerve-shattered flyers who had completed their fifty missions over Europe. Two Red Cross women (working under my brother) served each commandeered hotel, organizing "singe binges" (wiener roasts) and beer busts on the beach, and getting up fishing parties. My sister, having run away from home, worked as a barmaid and elevator operator at the Roney Plaza, lived with a zapped-out flyer for a while, was married to him for four months, and never saw him again. Once, driving down to Key West on the overseas highway in a borrowed car, he had to pull over to the side and stop and let her drive the rest of the way because the whumps the tires made on the concrete joints of the roadbed sounded so like the flak explosions he remembered over Germany. Men and women everywhere—a lot of the women with husbands overseas—took what love they could get from each other on a day-to-day basis, and then moved on.

The old morality was changing in Memphis too. The Southern girls were getting liberated, although they probably would not have used the word. He had a girl who worked in one of the defense plants. She lived at home with her parents and two sisters, who worked in defense plants also. No one in the family cared if he slept with her right there in the house just so long as she was on time for the next shift.

> I spent the last seven months of 1943 in the Memphis hospital. I was in love at least six times. I learned a lot about living on the home front. When I was shipped back out marked for Limited Duty, my four thousand dollars was gone and all I had to show for it were two tailored tropical worsted officer's uniforms with shoulder straps that I couldn't wear on the post. That, and a lot of memories. Memories I didn't want particularly. It was during a period when nobody wanted to remember things.

When I was a small boy in these years, my father used to take me up to Memphis to see the Ole Miss football games at Crump Stadium in the fall, or the Chick baseball games in the summer. We stayed right down the way in the old Chisca Hotel. We might easily have passed him on Union Street, or in the lobby of the Peabody where we came to look at the crowds, or in Forrest Park by the river where they and their girls had their boozy picnics. Once, years later, in the farmhouse in Sagaponack when we were talking about Memphis and I was trying to help him remember the name of some streets, I mentioned this to him. "Well, I don't think you'd have liked me too damned much then," he said.

When he was transferred to Camp Campbell, Kentucky, Nashville was their liberty town, but since he was pretty broke, life there was not so flamboyant as Memphis had been. Several months later, in July of 1944, he was mustered out of the Army. He was living alone in the cabin outside Asheville, North Carolina, when he heard the news that the war had ended. He had started working on a novel.

4.

Three people came into his life: Lowney Handy, Maxwell E. Perkins, and Burroughs Mitchell.

Lowney Handy, a strange, driven woman passionately devoted to literature and writing, was living in Robinson, Illinois, with her husband Harry, who was superintendent of the Ohio Oil Company refinery there. She had been the oldest of six girls in a family of nine children, and her father was the sheriff in Marshall, a small town twenty-five miles from Robinson. She was something of the school rebel and spent a great deal of time with her father's prisoners; her father kept them in the family house rather than the jail so they would not become hardened criminals. When she married Harry Handy and moved to Robinson, she found she was unable to have children. She wrote a novel that was immediately rejected. Then she thought back to her years in the jail and, to the consternation of her social set, she began helping the unmarried mothers and juvenile delinquents and alcoholics of Robinson. When the war came she started corresponding with servicemen and entertained them on their furloughs.

Jim had gotten a month's leave from Camp Campbell. He went back to Robinson in late 1943 and moved in with his Aunt Sadie. He was drinking heavily and thinking about going over the hill, and this prompted his aunt to introduce him to Lowney Handy. "You should have seen him then," Lowney said later:

> He swaggered; he wore dark glasses; he even asked me to read his poetry aloud. He had obviously come over for a free drink. Then he saw my books. We have books everywhere in the house, in the living room, even in the bathrooms. Jim got out of his chair and began to take down the books. He flipped through them and plopped them back as if he were gulping down what they had in them. So I asked him if he'd like to see my writing room. It's lined with books. He went from shelf to shelf. Then he picked out a couple and sat down on the floor with them, and I might as well have been in the next county. I just stood there and looked at him. The chip on the shoulder was gone. The poor guy. The poor lost guy.

"Jim's edges are so rough," she told someone later, "he's almost painful to associate with."

She was an attractive woman, and although she was almost eighteen years older than he—she was thirty-nine, he was twenty-two—they began an affair that lasted well into the 1950s, more or less with the knowledge of the husband. Harry Handy must have been an understanding soul, because when Jim was medically discharged from the Army he moved into the Handys' house in Robinson, into a study they fixed up for him in the back, and Harry helped him buy a jeep and trailer. He would drive the jeep and trailer all over the country—Arizona, the West Coast, Memphis, Florida—and settle in somewhere for a spell and write on his first novel, and Lowney would leave Robinson and meet him. She encouraged him in his writing and made him elaborate reading lists.

In the late forties Lowney set up a colony in Marshall called the "Handy Artist Group." (In 1951, when the money from *From Here to Eternity* started coming in, he became the sole financial backer, and more or less ran the place along with Lowney.) The writers lived on a 400-acre farm which the Handys owned near Marshall. In the winter she would rent a couple of cottages in Florida and take her fledglings down there. She furnished typewriters and writing supplies to the writers, three meals a day and a little spending money, and she spurred them on in unusual ways, sometimes getting them to type out whole sections of books such as *War and Peace* and *Madame Bovary* to show them that writing was not a trade for malingerers. She would put a new arrival through what she called the Treatment—doing all the dirty work, speaking only when spoken to; he was even forbidden to eat meat. If the would-be writer survived a month or so of this, he became an accepted member of the Group. "We've got no room for *artistes,*" she would say. "The first guy who tries to grow a beard is going to have a fat eye to go with it"; she was a good athlete, and it was not beneath her to startle one of her charges with a swift uppercut when she felt like it. No one was allowed to talk in any detail about his own work. "Too many writers talk themselves right out of writing their books," she said. Several years later, when Jim Jones became famous,

A. B. C. Whipple came out to write a piece for *Life* on him
and the colony and described this scene:

> Suddenly, like a flight of pigeons, the Group
> whisks down the beach to Nettie's Restaurant for
> spaghetti, in honor of something or another, and a
> loud gabble about writing takes place through the
> spaghetti while Lowney complains, "You all eat like
> hogs." Occasionally somebody gets a little too eso-
> teric and makes the mistake of mouthing something
> like "Well, after all, what's life and experience all
> about, anyway?" An immediate hush falls over the
> Group until he apologizes. "If you want to be a long-
> hair, you can leave now," she says.

His novel was called *They Shall Inherit the Laughter*—"a
youthfully bitter title," he would write later, "but apt." He
started it in Marshall and then rewrote it in New York City and
rewrote it again all through 1945 in the Florida Keys while
working on a commercial fishing boat. After he wrote it the
first time, he took his maiden trip to New York City and
carried the manuscript in a box tied with string to the offices
of Scribner's on Fifth Avenue and Forty-eighth Street to present to the legendary Maxwell E. Perkins, who he knew had
been Wolfe's Foxhall Morton Edwards—"the Fox"—as well as
the editor of Fitzgerald, Hemingway, Anderson, and Lardner.
A long two-part profile by Malcolm Cowley had appeared in
The New Yorker the year before about Perkins, who had always shunned publicity, and Jim may have seen that, but he
did not need to read it to have known of Perkins' great loyalty
and genius, and the immense role he had played in develop-
ing American talent and literature.

With the box in hand he went to the fifth floor and asked the receptionist if he could see Perkins. Mr. Perkins was not there, she primly said, but he could leave the box with her and the manuscript would get a reading. He was adamant—if Perkins would not see him, he would goddamned sure take his book somewhere else. The receptionist, possibly frightened by this stranger with the glaring eyes and the gruff voice, more likely than not smoking a cigar and carrying his knives in his ubiquitous satchel, disappeared down a hallway, then returned to say Mr. Perkins had just returned and would see him briefly. He went back to Perkins' office and found this eminence of American publishing sitting behind a desk with his hat on his head. Perkins began asking him about his Army experiences. They became very much involved in their talk about the war, and the subject of *They Shall Inherit the Laughter* was put aside. Finally Perkins said he would have a look at the manuscript later.*

Burroughs Mitchell, a Rhode Islander and a graduate of Bowdoin, came to work for Scribner's as a young man fresh out of the Navy and, in fact, still in his uniform; after Perkins' death the following year he would become, in turn, one of the fine editors of his day. One of the first manuscripts he read was the tenacious *They Shall Inherit the Laughter*. Both Perkins and John Hall Wheelock, Perkins' closest colleague at Scribner's, read the novel, and they all felt it was too clumsy

* In these pages on his early relationship with Perkins and Scribner's, I am drawing heavily on A. Scott Berg's invaluable account in his biography *Max Perkins: Editor of Genius*—as well as on Burroughs Mitchell's recollections and my own conversations with Jim Jones.

and uneven, but that it did show signs of a writer's power.
The main character was a soldier gone AWOL during wartime who had returned to his hometown and gone a little ber-
serk. The protagonist was guided around a bookstore by a
woman zealously devoted to literature—a Lowney Handy
figure. "That chapter was a sort of catalogue of great books,"
Mitchell would remember, "long-winded and naïve, but kind
of touching."

Perkins himself had found much to admire in the novel; the
author himself had also favorably impressed him. "It is a serious attempt to do a big piece of work and the author has the
temperament and the emotional projection of a writer," he
wrote. But he did not feel he could make an offer.

When Perkins rejected the novel, Lowney Handy came to
New York City from Illinois and persuaded Jim to enroll in a
couple of writing courses at NYU. He quit after three months
and took his jeep and trailer to Florida. He spent eight
months rewriting the book, and submitted it again in early
1946. "I have a number of plans I'm champing to get into action," he wrote Perkins, "and all of them hinge on this book,
whether it is accepted or rejected, whether you will consider
that it needs more work (personally, I'm sure it doesn't, but
it's just possible my judgment may be biased) and of course
the money angle, how large an advance and how soon. I'm
stony broke right now."

Perkins was much more intrigued by the covering letter
than he was by the revised manuscript. The author mentioned
that he wanted to write his next book about life in the peacetime Army, ending up with Pearl Harbor; he wanted to write
about the hate and frustration and humor of the thirty-year
man through two characters named Prewitt and Warden. In
February 1946 Perkins wired his prospect in Robinson, offer-

ing a $500 option on the new novel about the peacetime Army. "Wish to co-operate," the telegram said, "but have more faith in second novel and have further revision to propose for *Laughter*."

"My vanity was hurt and I didn't want to throw the first book away after all the work I had put into it," he remembered. "But I knew the story of F. Scott Fitzgerald and Thomas Wolfe and how Max Perkins had taken chances and worked wonders on their first novels." After a couple of days he wired back: "Placing myself in your hands . . . Wire $500 anytime." (Eventually, after he had finished *From Here to Eternity* four years later, he went back and read his unpublished book. "Parts of it actively embarrassed me, they were so bad," he said, and he burned it. But in it were the seeds of two later novels, *Some Came Running* and *Whistle*.)

At first he did not want to discard *They Shall Inherit the Laughter*. But finally he wrote Perkins:

> I trust your judgment from past knowledge of your work and your tremendous experience with such things that I don't have. And I'm willing to ride along . . .
> I think you probably know a lot more about it than I do, which is why I'm willing to lay it aside for Prewitt. As I said, I'm putting myself in your hands, not Scribner's exactly, but you personally, because I have more faith in your ability to see further and clearer than anybody I've met or heard of in the writing game.

Perkins was eager about the new novel; he expected a postwar literary movement. "I don't know that the form of the novel will change much," he wrote Jim, "but the spirit and the expression will. Some sense of direction will come in young men who are real writers, almost unconsciously, and as it does, they will formulate it." Also, if a writer worried too much about plot, he might become "sort of muscle bound," but he must be flexible. "A deft man may toss his hat across the office and hang it on a hook if he just naturally does it, but he will always miss it if he does it consciously. That is a ridiculous and extreme analogy, but there is something in it."

That letter, Jim remembered, "made me feel like one of the boys. That did it." He set himself to the long, difficult task of writing *From Here to Eternity*. "Max was like an old-time druggist," he said. "Whenever he saw you getting sluggish, he prescribed a book that he thought would pep you up. They were always specifically selected for your condition, perfectly matched to your particular tastes and temperament, but with enough of a kick to get you thinking in a new direction." He and Perkins had several private meetings. Perkins gave him advice from Hemingway. "Always stop while you are going good. Then when you resume you have the impetus of feeling that what you last did was good. Don't wait until you are baffled or stumped." He also wrote him:

> I remember reading somewhere what I thought was a very true statement to the effect that anybody could find out if he was a writer. If he were a writer, when he tried to write, out of some particular day, he found in the effort that he could recall exactly how the light fell and how the temperature felt, and all the quality of it. Most people cannot do it. If they can do it, they may never be successful in a pecuniary sense, but that ability is at the bottom of writing, I am sure.

In July 1946 Jim sent several chapters to Perkins, who replied:

> I do not know whether this book will sell, and I think there will be a very hard struggle in cutting it and shaping it up, but I think it exceedingly interesting and valid. The Army is something and I don't think anyone ever approached presenting it in its reality as you have done. I think though that one reason it needs a great deal of cutting is that you explain too much. You give too much exposition . . . When you come to revise, you must try to make the action and talk (which is a form of action) tell us all, or almost all.

Jim would remember the pain of these words about revising: "They stuck like a barb in my ass." But Perkins' counsel was working. "Eventually something happened in my head," he would remember. "The concept of a paragraph came to me for the first time. I realized the power I held to raise or lower a reader's emotional level by where I ended a paragraph."

Perkins died in June 1947. As the ambulance attendants were taking him away to the hospital, he instructed his daughter to take the two manuscripts by his bed and put them in his private secretary's hands, "and no one else's." The manuscripts were *Cry, the Beloved Country* by Alan Paton and the early chapters of *From Here to Eternity*. Not until John Hall Wheelock wrote Jim several days later did he know Perkins had died. He wrote Wheelock:

> I have had the feeling for a long time that I should come to New York, that he might die, that I should not selfishly but for writing go where he was because

there was so much that I could learn from him. But
as I said, life does not ever put two such things together; his time of that was with Thomas Wolfe and
not with me.

For days Jim kept remembering that phrase that brought him
to writing: "O lost, and by the wind grieved, ghost."

Burroughs Mitchell took over the editor's job on *From Here
to Eternity*. It was a fortuitous but happy match. Mitchell—
"Mitch" to his friends—had a splendid feel and discipline for
the language, and was a man of quiet courage, loyalty, and integrity, a literary man in the best sense, which were qualities
his author badly needed at this time.

From what I would know of him years later, I can surmise
his mood and his habits in those arduous months. His persist-
ence would have bordered on the stubborn, almost the recalci-
trant. He would have gone at the book in what I can only call
waves—one typed paragraph, then the same paragraph
rewritten and followed by another, then another page and
three paragraphs constantly rewritten, and the book would
have grown one layer after the other. He would have had pe-
riods of intense labor, and then have gotten away from it all
for a while. His own faith in the work would have been enormous. He would have read sections out loud to people he
trusted. He likely would have seduced more than a few
bookish girls in his trailer reading from selected passages,
especially about Sergeant Warden and Karen Holmes.

He must have loved America, even after everything: Robinson and Schofield, Guadalcanal and Memphis—its diversity
and sadness, its beauty as it unfolds on this continent. In his
drives in the jeep and trailer, working on his book wherever
he put down in the late 1940s, he must have felt the cry we

make for it as young men, the things Thomas Wolfe wanted us to believe and feel of America, that its own discovery yet remains for us; understood, too, what Fitzgerald sensed about the first Americans seeing its green coastline and facing then something commensurate with their capacity for wonder. He knew much about its complexity, and he would put something of this into his work, this and his perception of rootless, homeless American types, traveling the land in search of—what?—"this broad expanse of country that was called America which he loved deeply." Years later, in *Some Came Running*, he would write about the young man Wally from a small Illinois town, doomed to die with a throat slit by the Chinese infantrymen who swarmed the American emplacements on a frozen hill in Korea, his throat cut with his own knife by an enemy who outnumbered him, and then laughed at and mocked him. Before he was killed in this way, the boy from southern Illinois would think to himself in the last charge:

> They want what we got, was the phrase that always jumped into Wally's head as he squinted through the sights at targets. They want what we got. Our bread, our food, our guns, our ammo, our grenades, our warm clothes. And more than that they want all of that that we've got behind us back home: the luxuries they've never dreamed of: the richness of America: they want what we got, he would think, and fire. And we want to keep it, and that's why we're here: we mean to keep it. We built it, we made and invented it, why shouldn't we want to keep it? Squint and fire. Squint, and fire. Pick your targets. Don't waste ammo. Squint and fire. And still they kept coming . . .

Eventually he came up to New York for his first meeting with Burroughs Mitchell. Much later he told Mitchell that walking from Grand Central to the Scribner's office on Forty-eighth he had to stop twice to take a leak out of nervousness.

While *From Here to Eternity* was under way, he and his new editor wrote each other many letters, including a long discussion of all the nuances of sin. Jim traveled to New York several times from wherever he had been living in his trailer to confer with Mitchell.

> On one occasion my wife and I went with Jim to a Fifty-second Street jazz place called Jimmy Ryan's which he had been haunting. He brought over to our table the great Sidney Bechet, a quiet man with self-assurance and dignity. When Jim was away from the table, Bechet said to me: "Jim says he's writing a great book. And I believe him."
>
> In these days Jim carried a small black notebook in which he recorded sights and sayings that interested him. My remark that women rule the world (made at 3 A.M.) went down in his notebook and became my only contribution to *From Here to Eternity*.

While he was living in Naples, Florida, in the winter of 1948, he was "so written out, busted up, and worn down" from the novel that he took some time off and wrote a few short stories. One of them, "A Temper of Steel," became his first published work. It was taken by Edward Weeks, the discerning editor of the *Atlantic Monthly,* and run as an "Atlantic First," and later became part of his short story collection, *The Ice-Cream Headache.*

The following summer he went back to Memphis and was working on the stockade section of *From Here to Eternity*. He

had just brought in the character Jack Malloy—Prewitt and
Maggio's friend and mentor and the nemesis of Fatso Judson
—and was rereading everything he could get his hands on in
the libraries about the Wobblies; he could not get back to the
novel until he had finished this reading. He began a short
story then called "Greater Love," which was his first serious
attempt at writing about combat. Much of this story is directly
autobiographical, about the days he served on a grave regis-
tration detail on Guadalcanal, after the fighting had stopped
for a while, to dig up the bodies of the dead and bring them
back down to the main cemetery. The dead were soldiers
from another regiment, since the officers did not want them to
dig up men they might have known:

> Unfortunately, a man in my outfit on the detail
> had a brother in the other outfit, and we dug up
> the man's brother that day.
> It was a pretty awful scene. In any case. Even
> without the man's brother. The GRC lieutenant in
> charge had us get shovels out of the back of one of
> the trucks, and pointed out the area we were to
> cover, and explained to us how we were to take one
> dogtag off them before we put them in the bags. He
> explained that some of the bodies were pretty ripe
> because the fight had been two weeks before. When
> we began to dig, each time we opened a hole a little
> explosion of smell would burst up out of it, until
> finally the whole saddle where we were working was
> covered with it up to about knee deep. Above the
> knees it wasn't so bad, but when you had to bend
> down to search for the dogtag (we took turns doing
> this job) it was like diving down into another ele-
> ment, like water, or glue. We found about four bod-
> ies without dogtags that day.

"What will happen to those, sir?" I asked the lieutenant. Although he must have done this job before, he had a tight, screwed-up look of distaste on his face.

"They will remain anonymous," he said.

"What about the ones with dogtags?" I asked.

"Well," he said, "they will be recorded."

A fellow who had been in Guadalcanal and New Georgia had moved in with a trailer down the road in the Memphis trailer park. They would talk about their time in the Pacific "sitting out at night on the porch beside his trailer or mine, breathing the night air and drinking beer." A little later the Hollywood people were filming Faulkner's *Intruder in the Dust* down in Oxford, Mississippi, eighty miles away. A friend of his who was studying on the GI Bill wanted the two of them to go down there and meet Faulkner. "I didn't want to," he said later. "Hell, I loved the man's work, but I knew he didn't want to be bothered." Years after that, he and Gloria saw Hemingway alone late one foggy night in the Piazza San Marco in Venice; Gloria wanted to go up and say hello, but he said, "Hell no, leave the man alone."

Finally, in August of 1950, he finished *From Here to Eternity* and sent it off to Burroughs Mitchell in New York. The problems Scribner's had on the language were not unlike the problems Maxwell Perkins and Ernest Hemingway had sat down to a generation before on *The Sun Also Rises*, except on a larger scale entirely. "Mitch" remembered it:

> I said to Jim in a letter that he had written a great book—something that I've not said to any other writer. We did a certain amount of trimming of the manuscript and clarifying here and there, but the big

job didn't come until the lawyers had read the galleys. Remember, at that time Mailer had found it necessary to use the word *fug* in *The Naked and the Dead*. The lawyers argued, reasonably enough, that the great number of fucks and shits, while perhaps not actionable, would weary and prejudice a judge and a jury. So we were given an arbitrary number to cut out, along with some other troublesome details. We kept a scorecard of each day's work in the Scribner office—so many fucks and shits deleted that day.

It was very hard work; Jim's ear was so exact that you couldn't easily remove a word from the dialogue or substitute for it. But he kept doggedly at it, and eventually he began to treat the job as a puzzle, a game, and was delighted with himself when he found solutions. It was characteristic of him, then and afterward, that when an editorial decision was made, a look of anguish would come over his face, he would get up and pace, and finally he'd either accept or say, "I just can't change that," looking even more anguished. Finally I reported to Mr. Scribner that we had cut all the fucks we could cut, although not the lawyers' full quota, and Mr. Scribner cheerfully accepted the situation. That was certainly part of the reason why, when Charles Scribner died suddenly, Jim insisted on going to the funeral. He said he knew that Mr. Scribner had been worried about *Eternity*— but he had gone ahead and published it.

The book was published in 1951, when he had not yet turned thirty, and was a stupendous critical and financial success, a record-breaker, "a final confirmation of Max Perkins' gift," as A. Scott Berg would write, as it was of Mitchell's steadfast faith. The New York *Times* called it "a major contribution to our literature." It was number one on the best-seller list for five months and a Book-of-the-Month Club selection; it won the National Book Award for fiction, and eventually would be translated into three dozen languages. The paperback would sell into the millions. Overnight, as such things happen sometimes in America, the author was both rich and famous.

His whole life would change now—and then again it would not change much at all. He found it intriguing that when *From Here to Eternity* was published, he had five short stories on hand and within four months sold four of the five to magazines which had rejected all five at least twice. "I don't know what this signifies," he said later. One sour note was *Time* magazine's year-end roundup of books, which said that as usual in the postwar years, American fiction in 1951 had witnessed a general decline. Three especially disappointing works to the *Time* critics were *From Here to Eternity*, *The Catcher in the Rye*, and *Lie Down in Darkness*.

John P. Marquand, Jr., remembered meeting him shortly after the publication of *From Here to Eternity*. (Marquand was working on his own novel, *The Second Happiest Day*, under the name John Phillips.) His father, John P. Marquand, was a judge on the Book-of-the-Month Club and highly enthusiastic about *From Here to Eternity*. Scribner's had run teaser ads beginning three or four weeks before the publication date, with quotes from the elder Marquand and Norman Mailer.

Mr. Marquand had written Jim in Marshall, Illinois: "Your book hit me where I live." He arranged a luncheon for Jim at his apartment on East Sixty-seventh where some of the Book-of-the-Month Club people—Harry Sherman, Meredith Wood, Clifton Fadiman, Henry Seidel Canby—could meet the new author. Johnny Marquand was at the luncheon.

> They'd all heard these rumors that he was a kind of noble savage. They all wanted to meet him. Jim came into the room with all these older men. He was looking at them, they were looking at him. I remembered it as a cultural collision. They told him how much they liked his book. He had two or three martinis and loosened his tie. He was like a cowboy trying to behave, not to fuck up. He was very impressive. My father suggested the book should have ended with Prewitt's death. Jim disagreed; he defended his concluding pages eloquently. He told stories that day, such as about getting drunk on Guadalcanal on the fermented booze and the soldier who reminded him of Prewitt who crawled on the ground and bayed.

Jim and Johnny Marquand did some walking around the city. "I went with him to a lot of places—to bookstores, to Dunhill, to Abercrombie and Fitch. He was buying books on ballet, expensive pipes, and guns and knives. He was like an Indian in Oklahoma when oil's been struck."

William Styron, who would later become one of Jim's closest friends and along the way one of America's greatest novelists, first met him in the fall of 1951 in New York City through Johnny Marquand. Young Marquand took Styron to another small party Mr. Marquand was having for Jim at the apartment on the East Side. Styron, a Virginia boy who grew up on the banks of the James River, attended Christchurch School, and studied under William Blackburn at Duke, had just gotten out of the Marines, and was living in the Village; *Lie Down in Darkness* had just been published to much acclaim. He was a comic, serious, deeply intelligent young man—his intelligence and feeling so Southern in their roots, derived of a love for the landscape of the Old Dominion, and the great and indomitable resonances of its past. When I came up to New York in the early 1960s and we got to be friends, I once asked him what the words to Sir Thomas Browne's *Urn Burial* meant, the ones he put in front of *Lie Down in Darkness*. "They mean we're all in it together," he said, "and we're all in for a tough time." He had previously been fired, after an earlier stint in the Marines, as a junior editor at McGraw-Hill for having let loose some balloons out an open window, which drifted back into his boss's office—Mr. Edward Aswell—that and for his written opinion of the manuscript *Kon-Tiki:* "Who wants to read about a bunch of scruffy Norwegians in a dirty little boat?" All this would someday work its way into the opening pages of the big, tragic novel he would be writing, *Sophie's Choice*.

At the party at John Marquand's, Styron would recall, the guest of honor was in the company of a high-class stripper— "a very funny, nice gal, buxom and all woman."

> I was sort of envious of him. He was a very big public figure, immensely celebrated. He had already gotten into his tailored suits. One thing that always caused me to have an enormous affection for him was his body love for good things, tactile things, including clothes. He was already dressed in the best. I was still dressed in bags. I had a genuine admiration that night for the man's style, the way he honestly enjoyed the adulation he was getting.

Styron began to see more of him that fall and winter. In those days there was a great sense of excitement about quality literature in America. It was the postwar years, after the Hemingway, after the Faulkner generation, after the twenties. Vance Bourjaily had a kind of salon for literary people at his place in the Village. After one of these parties Jim Jones, Norman Mailer, Montgomery Clift, and Styron went to a little place off Sheridan Square, a rowdy local Italian bar, and sat drinking for a while. *From Here to Eternity* had just been bought by the movies for $82,000, but had not yet been cast. Styron remembered Jim saying to Clift, " 'I want you to play Prewitt.' The men at the bar didn't know who the hell anyone else was, but they knew who Montgomery Clift was, and they began to make remarks and to shout at him—things like 'What was it really like to screw Elizabeth Taylor?'—and since he was somewhat neurotic and shy he got very nervous, and all the while Jim was tapping him to play Prewitt. He was very pleased. Clift said he wondered whether he could play a fighter, and Jim said he sure as hell could."

Not long after the publication of *From Here to Eternity*, Burroughs Mitchell went out to visit Jim in Marshall, Illinois, at the colony. That was his first encounter with the redoubtable Mrs. Handy.

> She could be charming, easy, and warm; but her black eyes could quickly become blacker, her voice strident, with a violent outburst. Lowney was convinced she could do anything. She held various mystical beliefs, drawn from dubious books on Eastern thought (and some of this unfortunately affected Jim in *Some Came Running*). In Jim Jones, dedication to the art of writing was an essential part of a steadfast nature. In Lowney, that dedication was an obsession,

70

a madness. She had read quite widely, but unevenly. For example, she admired Arnold Bennett, but thought Dickens wrote stories for boys. She became a torment to Jim and ultimately went mad and committed suicide. But it has to be remembered that she gave him support and encouragement at the beginning of his career, when he was otherwise alone.

At the colony, he was living in a new, luxurious trailer, on a grassy hillside under the shade of three maples, surrounded by pipes, hats, Indian jewelry, beer mugs, books, knives, guns, and motorcycles. The eight or nine colonists all ate together as before, with Lowney doing the cooking.

Marshall was an old, settled town, not unlike Robinson twenty-five miles to the south. He had started *Some Came Running*, and the small Illinois town called Parkman which would be its setting was a blend of these towns, both physically and in spirit. Marshall was founded in the 1830s by a mixture of Kentuckians who came up the river from Evansville and Ohioans who arrived overland through Indiana. Some of them may have traveled up the Wabash in the company of young Lincoln when he came that way.

"The result of this admixture," he wrote in an essay during this period that he was living in Marshall, "is a town which is a curious combination of eastern frugality and taciturnity, and Southern laziness and easy-going living."

You can feel this strange mingling of two national types as you walk along the streets. The architecture of the courthouse, set in its square of big trees, is equal parts eastern plainness and Southern rococo. The same thing shows in the faces of the lounging farmers and businessmen on the sidewalks. It even

shows up in the local accent . . . wry nasality and
lazy drawl, almost impossible to reproduce on paper.

It was mainly a farming town then, drawing much of its business from the country people. On Saturdays they came in
from outlying hamlets like Bullskin and Darwin, Spiketown
and McKeen—"little communities of a few clustered houses
weathering away in sun-dappled shade among the trees on
high banks over the Wabash," or "flat little places on the endless prairies," with a heritage of violence from earlier days.

The town itself was graced with enormous oaks and maples,
their branches arched high over the wide, calm streets. There
were even older trees on the lawns of the brick mansions like
the Schofield house where Booth Tarkington's people used to
stay and where Tarkington played with the Schofield boys.
Penrod and Sam was written about Marshall and Tarkington's
childhood visits.

> Perhaps the first thing that really caught me, out-
> side of Marshall's oldness and its sense of perma-
> nence, was the humor. Not long ago, while my house
> was under construction, there was a national Legion
> convention in St. Louis. A bunch of the boys from
> the Marshall Post went over, all friends of mine.
> During the course of one of the many parties they
> made a point of bringing it out that they were
> from Marshall where "that Jim Jones that wrote that
> *From Here to Eternity* lives." The guys were
> impressed and wanted to know what he was like.
> "He's just a guy," one of the boys said, and I can
> hear that nasal drawl. "Just like anybody else. You
> want to meet him? That's him sittin' right over
> there."

72

James Jones at fifteen—Robinson, Illinois, 1936.
(Gloria Jones Collection)

Company F, 27th Infantry, Schofield Barracks, Hawaii—

November 1941, only days before the attack on Pearl Harbor.
(Gloria Jones Collection)

At Schofield Barracks, 1941.
(Gloria Jones Collection)

James Jones in his trailer camp. His job was moving trailers.
It was at this time that he was writing *From Here to Eternity*.
(Gloria Jones Collection)

Burroughs Mitchell, Jones's editor at Scribner's, with his
author, 1957.
(Gloria Jones Collection)

1951. At the time of publication of *From Here to Eternity*.
(Gloria Jones Collection)

James Jones and Montgomery Clift, 1954. Clift played Prewitt in the film of *From Here to Eternity*.
(Gloria Jones Collection)

With Edmund Trzcinski, author of *Stalag 17*, and Gloria
Jones in Portofino, Italy, 1959.
(Gloria Jones Collection)

With Gloria in Klosters, Switzerland, 1959.
(Gloria Jones Collection)

The girls were titillated and clustered around, and the member of the gang who had been indicated played the game along for an hour until they were all tired of it, giving out autographs and basking in the interest, while the whole gang of them laughed up their sleeves with that queer, quiet, peculiar country humor that I've not only come to love, but have also acquired a healthy respect for.

This could easily have been a scene in *Some Came Running*, with 'Bama Dillert as the main prankster.

On Burroughs Mitchell's second trip to Marshall, Jim was well into the novel. By then he had built his house on the outskirts of the colony, up in the woods—an expensive and impractical structure with a huge living room, a closet for a wine cellar, a large playroom with a Ping-Pong table, barbells, and punching bags, and an elaborate bathroom which had a bidet, quite possibly the only one in southern Illinois. Instead of chests there were drawers, hundreds of them, containing socks, shirts, handkerchiefs, ties, even cowboy hats and boots, all purchased in lots, as if he feared he would never get to a store again. One afternoon, Mitchell recalls, "when I was sitting outdoors reading and Jim was in the house presumably at work, I heard him laughing. He was reading a section of *Some Came Running*, and while he was laughing he was muttering something like 'that poor fucking fool.'"

Before Columbia Pictures began filming *From Here to Eternity*, Jim and Montgomery Clift stayed in close touch; Clift came to see him once when he was living in Arizona. After Clift signed for the part of Prewitt, he began studying and questioning his friend Jones. "All my girl friends said Monty Clift acted just like me in *From Here to Eternity*," he would recall.

In 1953 he went to Hollywood and wrote a first draft of the screenplay on the Columbia lot. Daniel Taradash, the screenwriter, shaped what became the final version. During the filming, Clift, Jim, and Frank Sinatra, who had more or less been rescued from a downslide in his career when he got the part of Maggio much at the author's urging, became inseparable friends. The three of them went out every night to an Italian restaurant in West Hollywood. Jim was disturbed that his version of the screenplay had been largely discarded and that such parts of the novel as the brutality in the stockade were not being used at all. He complained frequently to Clift and Sinatra about what he called the "ass-kissing" of the Army. The Hollywood people, he told them, were toning down the spirit of his book so they could shoot the exteriors on location at Schofield Barracks.

"We talked about the injustice of life and love," he told Patricia Bosworth for her biography of Clift, "and then Monty and I would listen to Frank talk about Ava Gardner. We would get very, very loaded. After dinner and a lot more drinks we would weave outside into the night and all sit down on the curb next to a lamppost. It became our lamppost and we'd mumble more nonsense to each other. We felt very close." Occasionally, when they came back to the Roosevelt Hotel where they all stayed they would throw beer cans out the windows. Clift, who had learned to play the bugle, sometimes sounded it outside his window. "He would wake people up playing taps," Jim remembered. The Columbia executives had to intervene twice to keep the three of them from being evicted. Often, after he had finished practicing his scenes with

74

Sinatra, Clift would come down to Jim's room and ask him all
about his childhood in Robinson and his life in the peacetime
Army.

> He'd come crawling down the fire escape, agile as
> a monkey, and then swing into my room. He'd be
> brandishing a bottle of scotch and a pot of espresso
> . . . We'd sit around and booze it up. I don't re-
> member much of what we talked about. Monty
> talked more than me. He was an odd man, but I felt
> a strange rapport with him while we were making
> the movie.
> I told him I felt cut off from a lot of experience
> being a writer, working by myself so much, and he
> said actors were cut off too. "Except you writers
> don't need to hear the sound of applause," he said. I
> said, "What the hell are you talkin' about?" and he
> stares at me with those funny blazing eyes of his and
> then he starts laughing that crazy-sounding laugh.

The movie came out in 1954 to superlative acclaim. Bosley
Crowther of the New York *Times* called it "a film as towering
and persuasive as its source."

5.

He continued to live in the colony in Marshall, and likewise continued to spend a large part of the money he made on *From Here to Eternity* to finance it. He also kept traveling around the country in his trailer, as he had done when he was writing *From Here to Eternity*.

Some Came Running took five years. It was one of the longest novels ever to have been published in this country, 1,266 pages. It was a majestic, encompassing book, in some ways his best—perhaps his most ambitious. It was massacred by the critics. Much later, when he moved to rural Long Island, he had a big cardboard box full of these bitter reviews. Many made fun of it and left it at that; *Some Came Running*, others said, proved that James Jones was a one-book man, not an infrequent phenomenon in American writing. It would be the most abused—and subsequently the most neglected—

great novel of twentieth-century American literature. A kind of imprimatur would come down on this novel. In the author's lifetime it would somehow get buried, as many great books do.

Burroughs Mitchell would remember those days:

> When *Some Came Running* was finished, I got Jim to do a good deal of cutting, but not as much as was needed. Again there was the problem of obscenity and the lawyers. One of them said that the novel, as it stood, would be brought to court in every state of the Union except Nevada, where there was no obscenity statute. I remember the morning Jim and I started to work in the small library of Scribner's, with that enormous pile of manuscript facing us. I said that we would just have to go step by step, day by day; we must not let the job overwhelm us. He said: "Well, I trust you."
>
> On publication, *Some Came Running* was attacked right and left. When J. Donald Adams in the *Times Book Review* implied that the book had been written solely to make money, Jim came into the office white with rage. He had the draft of a letter to Adams. I suggested some cuts in it; then we made some more cuts; and finally we threw the letter away. Later on, I had lunch with Adams. He seemed genuinely surprised that his piece was offensive.
>
> The criticisms—the charges of windiness and awkwardness—hurt Jim, although he said little. But *The Pistol*, at least partly, eventually grew out of it. He wanted to write a short book. He wanted the prose to be precise and grammatical; he told me to check the typescript carefully for any flaw in the use of the

77

language (and I found virtually none). He wanted
to show them, and he did.

"The lower middle-class boy-man, not soldiers as such,"
David Bazelon wrote, "was Jones's subject. The common American man is a great traditional subject, and Jones in his generation was probably its major caretaker." I believe, further,
that no one has written about middle-class America—about
what would later be called "middle America"—with the dis-
cernment and, moreover, with the *love* that he brought to
Some Came Running.

> The town was creeping back into Dave some way,
> powerfully, emotionally, inexorably, a powerful cur-
> rent carrying below its surface the jumbled slowly
> tumbling flotsam of dead uprooted memories.
> Watching the seasons change across its face had a
> great deal to do with causing it in him. He had never
> thought he would ever love this miserable, beautiful,
> backward-in-all-the-wrong-ways, progressive-in-all-
> the-wrong-ways, petty little Illinois town. But he did.

Compared with his character Frank Hirsch, one of the
major characters in *Some Came Running*, Babbitt and Dods-
worth and Kennicott become rather pale figures indeed. The
book is difficult to get into, much too long in places, and
flawed here and there by exaggerated prose, especially ad-
verbs, but when this is said, one would wish to challenge any
dispassionate reader to read Sinclair Lewis and Sherwood Anderson, and then *Some Came Running*. My claim here is
unabashed. It is the towering work of native social realism
that American writers once dreamed of writing.

Nor do I believe any American writer has created as authentic a portrait of what it is like to be a writer in this country as the character Dave Hirsch in *Some Came Running*. In fact, the comic war novel that Dave is writing actually presages *The Thin Red Line*, which among other things would be just that: a comic war novel, comic in the sense that irony is comic; few scenes in this later novel would be so horrifyingly funny as the one in which the frightened American GI kills the equally frightened, emaciated Japanese soldier. This irony is pervasive in *Some Came Running*. Jim Jones was writing about the decline and fall of American society in the boom postwar years. Raymond and his brother and even the crazed stranger who kills Dave Hirsch are veterans warped and ruined by the war.

> It seems that in the last few years the crippled had become a normal part of everyday life, a steady stream of them, rolling back from over both seas; hardly anyone even noticed them anymore. He was suddenly reminded of Falstaff's speech about the maimed and crippled rabble, home from the Continental Wars. It must have been a lot like this in Rome too, during *her* great days. Except that now the government bought them cars which the taxpayers paid for.
>
> Sometimes, and increasingly the past year and a half that he'd served with the Occupation Army in Germany, Dave got the feeling he was living in a dying age. It was the same feeling he got when he listened to Stravinsky's *The Rite of Spring*, a picture not of the birth of the world but the death, and the now primitive tribes that sang hauntingly of the for-

mer greatness of their people and put the rusted gun
and the wrecked auto upon their stone altars and
worshipped them as gods because they no longer
knew how to operate them, while they sang to them
their haunting songs of a dying race.

Along roads and streets no longer plainly marked,
amongst courthouses and buildings turned into grass
grown piles of masonry, filled with the rotting papers
and unreadable records of an entire civilization,
gone.

And in Germany it was not hard to believe it completely. Here it was a little harder.

The reviewers often twitted the author for being unable to
create believable females. "Jones wrote nothing even remotely
convincing about women, but he wrote a great deal about
them, nonetheless," one writer said in 1978. The portraits of
Gwen, of Ginny, of Dawn, of Agnes, of Edith, and the others
give the falsehood to that notion. But it is greed and inso-
lence, the very qualities Solon identified as ruinous to Peri-
clean Greece, which are rampant. Women are cunning and
manipulative, men to a great extent romantic and foolish.
Even Frank Hirsch, the definitive portrait of the archetypal
small-town American businessman, has his romantic dreams of
glory, which may be what makes him so sympathetic. And
there are long sections which could stand by themselves as
vivid pieces of America: a small-town wedding, a poker game
in the American Legion hut, the country club, the low bar life,
sexual talk, life on a farm, and a drive from the North through
the South which is stunningly truthful of the differences between the regions, and high comedy as well. In this latter section, 'Bama Dillert gives Dave Hirsch a running commentary
and demonstration on the finer points of driving a car on

American highways that is as accurate as it is hilarious. It was written by a man who had done a lot of driving, and who knew the Great American Road.

Peter Matthiessen, then not quite thirty, was an Easterner and a Yale graduate with Virginia antecedents—a venerable plantation source near Tappahannock called Bladensfield, one of the oldest homes in Virginia, where his mother's people endured the Civil War with poetry, courage, and laughter, and near which his great-uncles died as teen-aged soldiers in their native fields. In the early fifties he had founded the *Paris Review*, a gifted young man of wide interests and intelligence. He was on his way to becoming one of the country's finest writers of prose as a novelist and a naturalist with such books as *At Play in the Fields of the Lord*, *The Shorebirds of America*, *Far Tortuga*, and *The Snow Leopard*. He would recall a big literary party in a hotel ballroom in New York City not long after the publication of *Some Came Running*—the National Book Award splash for all the out-of-town book reviewers. In the middle of it was Jim, surrounded by curious, hostile people. As the flashbulbs popped all round, one of them wanted to know, from the author himself, why he had written such a horrendous flop after *From Here to Eternity*. Matthiessen, Bill Styron, and Jim, who had been sent to the party by their respective publishers, as young writers used to be in those days, sat at a dinner table that night with several of these reviewers. "They got their knives out on him in an incredibly nasty way," Matthiessen remembered. "I mean, really brutal. Bill and I told Jim he ought to tell them to go fuck themselves. He wouldn't do it. He didn't get ugly or abusive. He talked with them quietly about the book. I've written a great book,' he said simply. He was distinguished enough to take the attitude: Well, I think you're wrong, but let's discuss this. I was deeply touched by the way he talked with those people."

Herman Gollob, the New York editor by way of Houston and Texas A&M, was in Paris in the spring of 1960. He and Jim had dinner and then went back to his house on the Île. "Jones and I stayed up most of the night, shooting the shit, as they said at College Station. At one point, I began extolling *From Here to Eternity*, and it enraged Jones. 'You goddamned romantic fucker,' he said, 'you really like that romantic bull-shit. That's all it is. The only thing I've ever written that's worth a fuck is *Some Came Running*. That's what they'll remember me for. Nobody thought *The Red and the Black* was worth a bloody fuck when it was published. The same for *Moby Dick*. You wait. *Running* is what they'll remember.'" Gollob recalled one of the revealing quotes in the front matter of *Some Came Running*, from *Don Quixote*: "At last he had behind him his damnable books of Romance."

During the years that he was being published by Scribner's, he was often in Burroughs Mitchell's office.

It was obvious that he felt at home; he knew everyone and had them figured out. Once he remarked to me, approvingly, that there were no fat people on the fifth floor where the editorial offices were. He had a special affection and respect for John Hall Wheelock, which were returned. The distinguishing feature of Jack Wheelock, Jim said, was "gentle manliness." On Jim's visits he seldom sat down. He stood, he prowled, always on the lookout for a new book. When he found one, on whatever subject, he would rather sheepishly ask for it. In the later days he often dropped in with his friend Tom Chamales, who had been one of the writers at the colony and wrote a novel for Scribner's called *Never So Few*. Tom was a very large, powerfully built man ("If he fell on you, he'd probably kill you," Jim said) who moved gracefully, spoke gently, and had a soft, manic laugh. Filled with martinis after lunch, they would hover around my desk, telling some tale on each other, until Jim would say they had better let me do some work and they would depart, a formidable pair.

On one New York trip, in 1958, Jim became suddenly very occupied. Then one afternoon he asked my colleague Harry Brague and me to come around the corner to Cherio's for a drink. It was to meet a girl, and she was Gloria. She claims she was being put on inspection. But I think maybe we were.

She was Gloria Mosolino, a beautiful, busty blonde, from Pottsville, Pennsylvania, John O'Hara's hometown. Her great-uncle had been a well-known bandit in southern Italy. Her family was in the rackets, and another of her uncles was the bootlegger in O'Hara's *Appointment in Samarra*. She came to New York City after Syracuse University with the idea of going to law school, after having been an honor student and even a saxophone player in the Syracuse orchestra, but she taught dancing for a while at Arthur Murray's, and wrote a novel which was never published, and did a little acting, and was Eva Marie Saint's and Marilyn Monroe's stand-in in some movies. One friend remembered meeting her for the first time. "Jim had told me, 'I've found the girl.' Talking with her for the first fifteen minutes, I didn't know what in hell to think. After another thirty minutes she had me, I was hers forever."

Everyone would become Gloria's. Her generosity and kindness were to be legendary in Paris, and along with it her propensity for deflating pomposity and the earthy sustenance she always gave those with broken loves, or writers' blocks, or *Angst* in its wilder dimensions. It is important to hear her voice, which must have stunned her future husband on their first meeting: a husky, amused, insinuating voice, with the promise of warmth and confidentiality, and with the expectation of laughter always behind it. I never knew anyone who could make a disparate group of people so amiable together. "He was the first man who ever truly loved me," she said. Their marriage would be the first and last for them, and was of another order; I have never seen one quite like it. They were splendid together, and forlorn apart. They loved each other passionately, and she was fiercely loyal to him; she would have killed for him, and I have no doubt she longed to entice into the torture chamber more than one reviewer for lingering, gruesome deaths.

A player of the horses, a card shark, a drinker of scotch, a reader of literature, a judge of character equal to her husband, she was touched with a feeling of fun and mischief, and just as unpredictable. Once, years later, she left Jim in Miami and came up and stayed in my house in Bridgehampton while looking around for a place to buy. She missed her husband so much that after four days she lost her voice. One morning I came down and saw that the dirty dishes in my kitchen sink, an incredible pile of them, had vanished. I thanked her. "Don't mention it," she said—a little strangely, I thought. Later I found the dishes, still dirty, packed away in a plastic garbage bag in the closet. She also had a way, in moments of drama or tenderness, of coming out with things that she did not really intend to say, especially when she lived in Paris and was trying to use French, but sometimes, too, in English. One day in the Russian Tea Room in New York City she and Jim ran into an old acquaintance and asked how he was doing. Not too well, the man replied, and went on to tell them he had terminal cancer. Gloria wished to say how sorry she was, but somehow the words came out: "My God! Better you than me."

It was Budd Schulberg who brought them together. Schulberg, then forty-three, was well known for his novel of Hollywood *What Makes Sammy Run?* and for his autobiographical work of fiction *The Disenchanted* about his days as a very young scriptwriter working with Scott Fitzgerald in Fitzgerald's decline, ending with that nightmare of horror and laughter at the Winter Festival at Dartmouth. His screenplays *The Harder They Fall* and *On the Waterfront* were also widely admired. He had grown up in Hollywood and came East for the first time for his senior year at Deerfield. "I was so Hollywood, all I knew was movies, tennis, track, and boxing. When I got off the train in New England, there was a whole other world in America. It was so green." After graduating from Dartmouth, and not long after Pearl Harbor, he volunteered for the Navy and was an officer in the OSS. Later, at the Nuremberg trials, he was in charge of the photographic evidence for the prosecution.

Schulberg met Jim at a cocktail party at the apartment of Harvey Breit of the *Times Book Review* one night in 1958. "This Jones looked less like a writer than any of that strange tribe I had met. He was small but built large, with a barrel chest and lantern jaw and the craggy face I would put on an ex-drill sergeant or a tank-town middleweight. His vocab-

ulary was a string of four-letter words and, in the field of
current literary gossip, he was an ignoramus." After the party,
they went back to Schulberg's rooms in the Sulgrave Hotel,
drank a bottle of Jack Daniel's, and talked until dawn. "He
didn't use phrases like 'the human condition.' It was refresh-
ing. Most of my friends were used to worrying about the
human condition. Jim talked about Jim and the people he had
grown up with in Robinson."

At dawn Schulberg crept off to sleep, saying goodbye and
suggesting they get together again soon. But the next morning
he found his visitor sleeping on the living room floor. They
had bloody marys and stale Swiss cheese and saltines for
breakfast and fell into another conversation about women,
marriage, and infidelity that lasted into the afternoon. Schulberg showered and dressed and said he was going to meet a
friend. "Anybody I know?" Jim asked. "Faye Emerson,"
Schulberg said. "Oh, I've seen her on TV. I like her. Can I go
with you?" After the visit with Miss Emerson, he asked Schulberg where they were going next. "Okay, Jim, on we go . . ."

> Back in the Sulgrave pad next day Jim was dozing
> or meditating in the living room and I was getting
> ready to slip out again. But he caught me. "What've
> we got on for today?"
>
> It was time for a heart-to-heart talk. "Jim, I like
> you a lot—we really get along. But tomorrow's Mon-
> day. I've got to get back to work, I don't want to
> throw you out but—you like direct questions—what
> the fuck is wrong with you?"
>
> Jim looked at me in the eye and said, "I'm lonely."
>
> "What are you looking for?"
>
> "A woman. I don't mean just for tonight. I'm tired
> of catting around."

"What kind of a woman?"

"Well, she has to be interested in writers and writing, but don't give me one of the New York intellectual highbrows. Somebody who likes books without all that bullshit. Somebody who likes men in a sort of old-fashioned way and at the same time isn't afraid of four-letter words. A real woman, a whole person, and," he paused, "I'd like her to look something like Marilyn Monroe."

"Jim, you've just described a friend of mine. She just finished working in a movie in which she doubled for Marilyn Monroe. She's bright, she's voluptuous, she could give Carole Lombard a lesson in four-letter words, she's outrageous and adorable."

Halfway through, Jim was on his feet excited. "How soon can I meet her?" I called Mos—that was what we called her in those days—and told her I had a friend with me, a writer from out of town about thirty-five years old, who'd like to meet her. "Who is he?" "James Jones." There was a pause. "Will I like him?"

"Mos," I said, "take a deep breath, because that's what I'm doing. I've got a crazy feeling that you're going to marry him."

"I was a writer fucker," she remembers. "There was a group of us—writer fuckers."

I graduated in '49. Then there were good girls who didn't screw. But we all did: a gang of us I still see. The others are now two lady doctors, two lady lawyers. Sometimes you'd get in serious trouble and need an abortionist. I knew one in Pennsylvania who did them for $25 and I'd send everyone to him. He

was the nicest man, from Ashland, Pennsylvania. He
didn't do them for profit—he was a great humanist.
We were freewheelers. It was nothing to do with
being whores. We came to New York and decided not
to settle into suburbia with a boring husband. These
few girlfriends . . . we were the beginning for the
children of 1968. We broke the ice.

A torrid courtship followed. He showed up for their first
date dressed in boots and Indian jewelry and speaking in a
cowboy voice like Gary Cooper's. The painter Cecile Gray
(later to marry the composer Irwin Bazelon) had been
Gloria's roommate during all four years in college and now
shared with her a fourth-floor walk-up over a liquor store at
Park and Sixty-fifth which Gloria called "the only tenement on
Park Avenue." As a lifelong friend, she remembered that first
night.

Gloria was nervous. Jim was at the height of his
Eternity stardom and, naturally, it was exciting to go
out with a literary celebrity. We never considered he
too would be nervous. The tension was sharpened by
the fact that he arrived two hours and several drinks
late, making an entrance that could be called anything but auspicious. He climbed the steep apartment stairs out of breath and slightly tipsy. Mos was
elegantly dressed for a night on the town. Even Jim
was impressed by her beauty. That she was also intelligent, witty, and fun he could not have known on
first meeting her.

A couple of days later, Gloria got him to look over her unpublished novel, and he told her that it was third-rate O'Hara

and "pure bullshit." He said: "You better quit and come out to lunch with me." Where, at lunch, he said: "You keep yourself free for me. I have one more date and then we're never going to leave each other." Gloria remembered she thought this guy was nuts. "But he was right. We never did leave each other." He proposed to her at a table in the back room of P. J. Clarke's. Danny Lavezzo, the erstwhile owner of that establishment, who recalled that. day, promised later he would put up a plaque on the wall by the table.

"I knew by intuition that Jim was the right man for Mos," Cecile Gray said.

> We already knew by reputation that he was certainly not a Milquetoast with women, and Mos liked strong men. Moreover, they had common backgrounds—small-town upbringing, rebellion against small-town mores and family, and as it turned out truly common interests.
>
> Not that there weren't any problems. Jim was more than a little wary of women. In that six-week period before their marriage, both of them were nervous with each other, instinctively drawn together but terrified that the magic would wear thin. As a result, every time I turned around, the two were dragging me with them. Since I couldn't support myself as a painter, I was working then for a theatrical PR firm and the two of them would constantly appear at my office—to go to lunch or cocktails or to buy Jim some new clothes, to get rid of the Marshall, Illinois, "oh shucks" look he had at that time. And then, instead of staying at his hotel, he preferred to move into our apartment.
>
> Shortly after they met, she invited a battery of our

girlfriends to meet him. Our dearest friend was Addie Herder, the artist, who was a socialist in those days. Her first evening she spent arguing with him that people basically have altruistic feelings and need to find a basin in which to pour them. Jim argued that property and territory were the essential points and that people are basically selfish. This opinion and many other idealistic viewpoints which Addie and others of us had we came to share with Jim's more cynical appraisals of life. He was the keenest judge of human nature I have ever known. He saw the strengths and weaknesses in all of us as human beings and made the necessary allowances.

He had a lot of anger in him then, mainly when he was drinking. But as he matured he contained that anger, and to a large extent actually lost it. It was an emotion, however, with which he was on intimate terms and the verity of his writing about this basic characteristic was one of his many powers as a writer. He was a gentle and beautiful man, and I saw this even then. It was perhap this dichotomy between his tough exterior and his gentleness that made him so charismatic and so endearing.

After two or three weeks in New York, Gloria took him to the train to go back to Illinois. When he left, she started rereading *From Here to Eternity* and the galley proofs of *Some Came Running* which he had given her, and she said to herself, "God, this man *is* a writer." Soon he telephoned from Illinois and said, "All right, goddam it, get on a plane and come out here." She got on the wrong plane. She was supposed to go to Indianapolis, but she got a ticket to Minneapolis instead. Luckily, this particular flight to Minneapolis stopped in Indianapolis anyway. She happened to look out the window while the plane was on the ground and saw him at the bottom of the steps. He was motioning frantically and saying, "Get off here, goddam it!"

They drove to Marshall. He had not bothered to tell her about Lowney Handy, and Lowney, unsurprisingly, was not cordial. But the affair was over. Soon they flew to Port-au-Prince, Haiti, and checked into the Olafson Hotel, a hotel where many American couples go when they are in love. They were married by a black voodoo master who was also a judge.

"It was the beginning of the single best marriage I have ever known," Cecile Gray said.

> They both believed in the sanctity of the family and the home. They both in truth had old-fashioned American values and no matter how sophisticated they became, they never deviated from their own personal commitment. Jim was always in love with her, but he also trusted her completely. It was a trust that came with time and intimacy. As he let his guard down and became less wary, they became a unified spirit.

Numerous other outstanding men, immensely talented and driven to writing, have chosen to make disastrous loves, full of catastrophe, self-destruction, and the very invitation to death, almost as if they were courting as part of the awful price of their imaginative talent the hostility of a certain breed of the female number. It says something about Jim Jones that he pursued a girl of inestimable character, loyalty, independence, and courage like Gloria Mosolino of Pottsville; and if this is not an example for young writers, what is?

They got a lot of money from the sale of *Some Came Running* to the movies and lived for a time a hectic New York City life. But after a while he could not take it any more. "Get me out of here," he said to Gloria.*

* It was in this period that a postal worker named Maggio, who lived in Brooklyn, sued him for one million dollars for defamation of character in both the book and the movie *From Here to Eternity*. Jim, thinking a man named Maggio from the old company had been killed in New Georgia, used the name for his fictional character. The jury in Brooklyn federal court was read lengthy excerpts of the novel, four-letter words and all. Maggio lost the suit, and later the members of the jury came down and shook the author's hand and congratulated him.

6.

They moved to Paris in 1958; they would be there fifteen years. For the lively and substantial American community in Paris in that period, it was the Jones Years. It is hard to fit in this exotic time with a life that already included southern Illinois, Hotel Street in Honolulu, Pearl Harbor Day, the hills called The Galloping Horse, the Memphis hospital, commercial fishing off the Keys, house-trailers, Hollywood, and the writers' colony in the woods—more than enough for most men's lifetimes—but Jim Jones the writer held together these extraordinary fragments, and Jones the man took to Paris as country boys in America a generation or two ago used to take to the courthouse squares on Saturday nights. In his case, to rephrase the cliché, you could take the boy out of America, but you damned well couldn't take America out of the boy.

There was nothing new about Americans in Paris, of course, even with the Lost Generation after the First World War.

"Though the writers of the twenties sometimes made it sound as though they had personally discovered the city," Tony Allen wrote in his *Americans in Paris*, "there had in fact been a sizable colony there throughout the nineteenth century and in the years before the First World War."

> There were even Americans in Paris during the Commune of 1870, when revolution broke out and the city came close to starvation. They formed a group called the Hungry Club, and gathered regularly to dine on such delicacies as cat mince, rat, peas and celery, and shoulder of dog with tomato sauce.

There were great American writers living there then also. Henry James, as a young man, earned his living, as Hemingway would, as a newspaper correspondent. And long before that, a couple of pretty good writers named Ben Franklin and Tom Jefferson had dwelled there, although they were not exactly expatriates.

"Jim was a literary man in a particular kind of way," Irwin Shaw once said. "He didn't go to college, and he had what many writers who don't have a full formal education have—a somewhat exaggerated and romantic notion, drawn in great measure from the twenties' blossoming of American writing in Paris—Hemingway, more than anyone else. He grappled with the ghost of Hemingway all his writing life, excoriating him, mocking him, worried about what Hemingway meant to him —Hemingway and Paris were always linked in his mind. He knew from the beginning that he wanted to go beyond Hemingway, but I think he felt that to get there he had to retrace Hemingway's steps, at least part of the way."

It was the age of the Great Green Passport, when American

hegemony was in full flower. Although the days were gone when Thomas Wolfe, as he described it in *Of Time and the River*, could have a five-course meal and a half-bottle of Nuits St. George at Drouant's for less than two dollars, the dollar exchange was exceptionally favorable still—especially on the black market—and went a long way for those who liked to spend money, as Jim Jones did.

Not a few Americans had been in Paris in the late forties on the GI Bill—painters such as Larry Rivers, writers such as Terry Southern. With their ninety dollars or so a month allotment, plus incidentals for tuition and books, they were able to live quite well, and to travel occasionally to southern France or Spain or Italy.

Much of the vibrancy of the early fifties in Paris had come from a group of young Americans and their wives and girlfriends whose focus was a new journal, the *Paris Review*—an interesting and attractive crew, a few of them pursuing the specters of Hemingway and Fitzgerald, of Lady Brett and Jake Barnes, on the boulevards of the Left Bank and the old haunted expatriate cafes. They included Peter Matthiessen and his wife Patsy—who many years later would settle in the eastern stretches of Long Island—Bill Styron, Donald Hall, Terry Southern, Tom Guinzburg, Doc Humes, John Marquand, Jr., and later Bob Silvers. And there was George Plimpton, who had been the youngest editor in chief of the *Harvard Lampoon* and who already was well on his way to becoming one of the most unusual figures of his day, around whom many of the eclectic pieces of America would somehow seem to cluster. The older friend and patron of these youngsters was Irwin Shaw, and they also saw a lot of the black writers Richard Wright and James Baldwin.

Much of the policy of the *Review* was shaped in a hectic little all-night *boîte* in Montparnasse called Le Chaplain. Offices of a sort were later established in the basement of a publishing house and were largely inaccessible to the outer world. Since the private door to these premises could not be unlocked, after six in the evening the editors could only leave through a window above a large courtyard far below. The secretaries were a group of miscellaneous American college girls who were collectively referred to as "Miss Apthecker," since none of them had work permits and all were fugitives from French justice. Despite these obstacles the *Review*, which was sent home in bulk for distribution in the States, attracted both promising young American writers and a group of distinguished international contributors. Its "writers-at-work" interviews would become notable fixtures on the literary scene. It caught something of the flavor of that time in Paris before the larger influx of Americans in the middle 1950s. It was part of the continuing wave of creative young Americans who had contributed something to Paris over the decades, and given it a peculiar poignancy. But by the time the Joneses came in 1958, this group had almost without exception, for one reason or another, gone back home, and the *Paris Review* would be edited—ironically but with a certain poetic rationale—in the United States.

In his memoir *Paris! Paris!*, Irwin Shaw remembered the good days of the 1950s, "the exuberant years when American arms had won the war and American money was restoring the world":

> The uniforms of the United States Army, Navy, and Air Force, with all the old familiar campaign ribbons, were everywhere to be seen, and NATO, with its famed American commanders, was a com-

forting presence in the city, and France was a gallant and reliable ally, at least in the public prints, and the PX in the American Embassy dispensed New World bounty like maple syrup and refrigerators and duty-free bourbon to the deserving troops and diplomats and their deserving friends. Charles de Gaulle was an aging, rusticated general, writing his memoirs in lapidary prose in a tiny, forgotten village called Colombey-les-deux-Églises that one passed through in two minutes on the way to skiing in Switzerland.

I recall with affection my own introduction to Paris on an April morning in this period. Four of us had bought a 1927 slate-blue Buick touring car with buff fenders for fifty-five pounds from a Captain Buckley-Johnson with the view of traveling from Oxford to Rome via Paris. We christened this relic "John Foster Dulles." After our third and last flat tire near Dover, however, we gave up; one of our number lost the coin flip and returned to London to get our money back, and the rest of us proceeded by boat-train across the Channel. After a somber English winter with its late-morning sunsets, the warmth and beauty of Paris overwhelmed the senses; after the melancholy Oxford girls who sometimes neglected to shave their legs and, in the Mississippi description, bathed once a month whether they needed to or not, the Parisian women were stunning. The sounds and smells of the city from the little hotel on Rue Gît-le-Coeur were a joy to the spirit, and the lush gardens and boulevards and grand facades as I reveled in them then bedevil me to this day. There were American coeds in swarms and on the loose. In fact there were Americans everywhere, undiscouraged by the "Americans Go Home" signs painted on the iron bridges. In American Express, among the long lines outside the mail windows, college classmates and fraternity brothers and sorority sisters greeted one another with vivacious embracings, wild shouts, and hee-haws that echoed out into the Place de l'Opéra. It was my first true affair of the heart with a great city, and I could readily understand why anyone would care passionately to live there.

In a setting such as this, the confined, self-enclosed circle of American life in Paris, with its atmosphere of a small-town community in which everybody knew practically everybody else, must have suited the Joneses perfectly. Jim was working hard on *The Thin Red Line,* and at first he and Gloria lived in a small apartment on Quai aux Fleurs over an *épicerie* which had a telephone. The proprietors would come out and scream upstairs: "Monsieur Jon-as—Hollywood!"

In those early months in Paris, he and Irwin Shaw formed a close and abiding friendship, close as brothers. Their differences in background and personality complemented each other perfectly. Shaw, earthy and ribald, the established, sophisticated novelist, playwright, and *New Yorker* writer, author of some of the finest short stories in the language and of the best war novel of the European theater—*The Young Lions* —the former quarterback for Brooklyn College, the courtly, witty tennis player and accomplished skier, the chum of Hemingway who first introduced his friend to his future wife Mary in London during the blitz. Jones, the rough, two-fisted beer and whiskey man, the busted-down private from Illinois at Schofield, survivor of the South Pacific combat, author of the celebrated war book with the four-letter words. Yet they shared the heart's commitment to the language, undeterred by the pedants of the day, and they were at once products and expressions of World War II, of the great American involvement in those tragic and momentous years. In Jones there was the American rifleman taken by surprise with his pants down in *The Thin Red Line* and grappling hand in hand to the death, his death dance with the starving foe who startled him at the edge of the jungle. In Shaw there was the young American lieutenant-colonel who came upon one of the death camps in *The Young Lions* and screamed to the Nazis: "I'll shoot, I'll shoot you sons-of-bitches if you do anything against the Jews of this camp." They both saw the American Army in that war as a crucible of America, of its past and its future. They epitomized that generation of American men whose lives would never again be the same, just as America would never be. As men and as writers they had been scourged by that war, and it had shaped them irrevocably. What if Shaw had been a private in the 25th Tropical Lightning Division on Guadalcanal and Jones a combat correspondent with the 4th Infantry in France? Such speculation does not take one very far. They were not really all that different. They deserved Paris.

Irwin was then forty-four, a big, burly, dark-haired, handsome, Jewish-looking man much loved for his laughter and generosity and fascination with people—a writer's writer, both intellectually knowing and intuitive, a man of deep sensibility. His knowledge of America, beginning with his growing up poor in Brooklyn during the Depression, was awesome—its urban life, the theatrical and intellectual worlds, politics, sports, women, Hollywood—and equally impressive was his feeling for Europe, in its everyday nuance and in the complexity of its history. His expertise on the food and drink of a dozen countries was likewise notable. It was impossible for anyone to feel uncomfortable around him. One would doubt if anyone in the world had more admiring friends. There were

walking along. I said, "Hello, how are you?" She
turned around and said, "Go home to your mother,
junior." *Now*, if somebody said that to me, I'd be flat-
tered, and I could still go home to my mother. She's
still around, and she'd be delighted to have me. But
from that day on I've never approached a lady until
I'd know damn well she'd talk to me . . .

Consider the case of Stendhal. He only got one
good review in his whole life, from Balzac. Nobody
ever bought his books. He had to work as a low civil
servant to eat. In college I read *Tender Is the Night*.
The critics didn't like it. I thought it was the best
book Fitzgerald had ever written. The moral is:
Don't read reviews . . .

The first time he saw Paris was on the day it was liberated
—August 25, 1944—the most memorable day of his life, he
said. He was in a Signal Corps unit which was made up of
two cameramen, a driver, and himself. Their jeep was laden
with flowers given them by the people in the small towns on
their way to Paris, and they had a small store of apples and
vegetables and bottles of wine that were gifts from the
crowds. As they halted in the square in front of Notre Dame,
a soldier in the truck ahead of them looked up at the spires
and said, "And one month ago I was in Bensonhurst." They
were playing the "Marseillaise" everywhere. "There was blood
against some of the walls, and the next day they were piling
flowers there for the dead and everybody was kissing everybody else and there was a considerable amount of free wine."

He had come back to Paris to live in 1951 with his wife
Marian and his one-year-old son Adam. They had an apart-
ment on a street between the Invalides and the Eiffel Tower.
When the Joneses settled there, he and Jim managed to see

each other almost every day—for lunch at Lipp's or at a little Vietnamese restaurant on the Île St. Louis of which Jim was the main patron, for a drink at the Café Flore, a stroll around the Left Bank, an afternoon at the races, an all-night poker game. He would recall: "Jim's boyish capacity for enjoying life increased the pleasure of everyone in his company. Our holidays together in those years, on the Mediterranean, at Deauville, in London, Biarritz, the Alps, at the bullfights in Nîmes, were monuments to hilarity and comradeship, and there will never be a bitter account like *A Moveable Feast* to darken their memory."

There was not a single one of the prominent French writers whom the Joneses did not know at one time or another. Romain Gary was an intimate and honored friend, as was Françoise Sagan. Gary, handsome and erudite, with a highly American sense of humor, had been a French hero as a pilot in the war and was a close friend of André Malraux. Sagan gave them her farmhouse in Normandy, right in the middle of a forest of rhododendrons, at holidays and every Christmas; Flaubert had once lived there.

They met a number of French writers through their friends Clem and Jessie Wood. Clem Wood was a Philadelphia Biddle, a gracious, sensitive man who had written a novel, *Welcome to the Club*, a hilarious book set during the American occupation in Japan, where Wood had been stationed after the war. Because Clem and Jessie had children the same ages as the Joneses', they did a lot of family things together: birthday parties, Thanksgiving dinners, Sunday afternoons in the country or at the movies. They would spend vacations together in Klosters; in a village in the Vaucluse called LaCoste with a ruined castle which had belonged to the Marquis de Sade; on the Greek island Spetsai where the Woods had a house; and in Florence where they rented a villa one Easter and Clem would go with Jim to look at the Masaccio frescoes in the Brancacci Chapel; Jim once stood looking at them in silence, and whispered, "They do something to me."

They saw André Malraux from time to time. He was the lover of Jessie Wood's mother, the writer Louise de Villemorin. She and Malraux lived in a beautiful castle called Verrière outside Paris, and the whole Jones family used to go there frequently for lunches and dinners. One day they were sitting at the table at the Woods' house in Paris with a huge leg of lamb in front of them. The Woods—Clem and Jessie and their assorted children—had a big basset hound named Andrew who was always biting the children, knocking things over, and otherwise making himself obnoxious. He reached up to the table on his paws and grabbed the leg of lamb in his mouth. Jim and Clem Wood stooped down and tried to pull it away. A few punches to his jaw persuaded the dog to let go. Malraux had a strange kind of affliction, which sometimes caused his face to fall down on the table. He was also a nonstop talker. He did not notice any of the drama of the basset hound and the leg of lamb, nor did Louise de Villemorin. At the table the Jones and Wood children composed themselves. Jim put the leg of lamb back on the serving plate and wiped off the saliva with his napkin. Clem, who was carving, asked each child if he wanted a portion. "Yes, thank you," each of them said properly, while Malraux kept on talking.

But they were never really *au courant* with the French intellectuals, one reason being the language difficulties. Jim spoke a crude, workmanlike French, accentuated by his Copperhead country drawl, but it was never good enough to carry on a complicated conversation. (Later, on Long Island, I heard him speaking French to one of his female cats and thought he had something caught in his throat. It was the only time I ever heard him speak French, and it was incongruous for me, and reminded me of having once seen Humphrey Bogart dubbed in Italian.) Many of the French intellectuals visited the house they bought at 10 Quai d'Orléans, and were always greeted generously and with grace, but it was pre-eminently and always a very American establishment. "The fact that he never wholly learned French and had almost no close French friends," Irwin Shaw believed, "was one of the paradoxes of his life that might be explained by his fear of losing what his instinct told him was one of his greatest assets —his profound Americanness. He loved Paris, its streets, its buildings, its cafes, its ambiance, but he professed to hate the French. I don't think he ever went to a French theater or read a French novel, except in translation. He absorbed Paris, all France, through his pores, not through his intellect, and his attempt to come to grips with the French came out as a failure in *The Merry Month of May*. I think that French wit, with its cruelty and flippancy, offended him, and he felt French emotion was too easily displayed and was more often than not falsified."

Eugene Braun-Munk, who was his European editor, recalled that "the relaxed, nice folks in France loved them—the gaiety of their life—but they were not on the same wavelength with the French intellectual establishment. Jim was serious about his craft and its obligations. He liked truth and guts, but he didn't care if somebody made a joke about something. He didn't have that hierarchical, holier-than-thou attitude of many French intellectuals. Being relaxed and joking and very loose isn't a French quality." Jim felt strongly about the cynical nature of Europeans, their frequent and brutal wars through history, the facile anti-Americanism of the 1950s and 1960s, and whenever the radical French intellectuals would categorically criticize the United States, he would remind them that America had saved them twice in less than thirty years.

His feelings about France always remained contradictory, as this passage which he would later write reveals:

> The harsh fierce summers and harsh fierce winters of New York and Ohio would make cloud-covered France a melancholy place for any American. They wrote about the rain all through World War I. At least two generations of Americans have used French weather as a large part of their literary capital. Especially Northern France. Every kilometer north and east that you get from Paris you find the French more and more like the Germans: melancholy, alcoholic, therefore intensely military, big eaters of pig sausages against the long, gloomy, dull and chilly winters, big eaters of fats, big eaters period. And yet, after you've lived there long enough, you find those gray cloud-covered days no longer depress even that eternal and oppressive American optimism we have. The gray drizzly cloud-cover becomes a natural, and pleasurable, part of life.

"He wrote *The Thin Red Line* upstairs at 10 Quai d'Orléans," David Bazelon observed, "and that symphony in fear is the truest and the best American combat novel my wartime generation is ever going to read or write." Another critic would call it "the most authentic and sublimely compassionate book to come out of the pits of World War II."

Drawing on his Guadalcanal experiences was tough emotionally. Yet *The Thin Red Line* (taken from both the Kipling poem and from an old Midwestern saying: "There's only a thin red line between the sane and the mad") was to be, with the exception of his novella *The Pistol*, the most perfectly structured book he wrote, with the consistently best prose—clean, flexible, and incisive. Carrying the company from Hawaii to the 'Canal and through its brutal jungle fighting, he employed a ruthless irony to capture the lunacy of war, and in places his humor is as biting as anything he ever wrote. It is not surprising that many would consider this his masterpiece.

The concluding paragraphs of the novel are stunningly beautiful. Most of Guadalcanal has been secured. The old company has withdrawn from up the line. Gasping in the airless humidity, they are marching along the same beaches on which they had landed months before, toward the landing craft which will take them to the big boats and then on to the next island—presumably New Georgia. They see a soldier perched high on the prow of a wrecked Japanese barge watching them pass by. He is munching a fresh apple, and they wonder—where could that fresh red apple have come from among all the crates of dried, dehydrated foods? In the distance are the hundreds of crosses laid out in their rows in the new cemetery, set on a carefully manicured lawn now, with water sprinklers all around. Some of their buddies are buried there, brought back from the makeshift graves out in the bush. They ponder as they march what they have lived through, and why. *Property. Property.* All for Property, Sergeant Welch thinks again, feeling furtively for his two canteens of gin. "Well, this was a pretty good-sized chunk of real estate, wasn't it?" And the last sentence:

> One day one of their number would write a book about all this, but none of them would believe it, because none of them would remember it that way.

He had begun *The Thin Red Line* in the small apartment on Quai aux Fleurs, the one that was situated over the *épicerie*. One day he was writing the memorable scene in which a member of the company is badly wounded and stranded in no man's land, crying out for help, and Witt waits until nightfall and crawls out there to give him morphine, then crawls back; the next day they will find the boy there, dead, with several of the needles in his stomach.

While Jim was laboring on this section, there was a knock on the door of the apartment; it was the big fat wrestler who worked for the laundry coming to collect the laundry bill. The Joneses knew this fellow very well. Gloria was pregnant, and he thought they were poor struggling young Americans trying to get by in Paris. Jim answered the knock on the door with tears streaming down his face from the scene he was finishing. The laundryman thought he was crying because he did not have the money to pay the bill. The man said, "*Pas nécessaire* —It's okay. You no have to pay now."

A couple of years later they were about to leave their house for a trip to Yugoslavia with Marian and Irwin Shaw. Just as they were leaving, with the bags all packed near the doorway, Jim came down the stairs with the expression of hopeless despair he would sometimes get. Gloria asked what was wrong, and he said, "The fucking *book* is all wrong. I've got to start all over." He banged his head against the wall. There was a beautiful Picasso plate on the wall, a gift from his German publishers, and when he banged his head this valuable plate fell, barely missing him, and hit the floor and shattered into a hundred pieces.

Burroughs Mitchell would remember:

> This was the period when the Joneses seemed to be continually getting on and off boats, and I went down to meet their boat one morning. As Jim stepped onto the gangplank, he sighted me, and immediately began to talk about *The Thin Red Line*. Coming down the gangplank, he told me that he wasn't going to change one goddam word, no matter what the lawyers said. His position was fully clear by the time he set foot on American soil.
>
> The lawyers had nothing to complain about in that book. I did suggest some condensing of the descriptions of terrain, which were detailed enough to satisfy any military historian. Jim did the cutting in the Scribner office, and one morning I saw him still at work when I thought everything had been done. I inquired. "Gene Baro says there are some symbols in here," he said, "and I'm taking them out."

After *The Thin Red Line* was published in 1962, he inscribed a copy to his daughter:

> Biarritz
>
> To Kaylie—
>   On her 4th birthday. You may have to wait awhile for the next one. I'm afraid I can't keep up with you.
>   Love,
>   Daddie

7.

Bill Styron had first visited Paris in 1951, shortly after the publication in America of *Lie Down in Darkness*. He came with letters of introduction to Peter Matthiessen from John Marquand, Jr. Matthiessen took him to a restaurant high on the Left Bank called Ti-Jos, for the Belon oysters. Styron had some wine and became homesick. He had arrived ahead of his reputation and felt, no doubt, a little lost. "What am I doing in this strange city?" he asked Peter. "I'm going back to the James River and raise peanuts. I ain't got no more resistance to change than a snowflake." The same thing happened to him when he later went to Rome; he wrote Matthiessen to say that on one of these drunk, homesick evenings, he lay down in the gutter, "where the children pelted me with grapes."

He grew to love Paris, however, and he and his wife Rose, who had put down roots in Roxbury, Connecticut, always stayed at the Jones house on the Île St. Louis on their many visits:

> What I recall most about those Paris days was two people enjoying life to the utmost. I say that with all the reservations implied in such a statement, which anyone should be able to divine. It was a chic life— but controlled chic. They had staked out a life of enormous zest and fun. I don't mean hedonistic, because it involved hard work too. But they truly were people who loved what they were doing and the place they were in and the friends who were there.

In the twenties Hart Crane once wrote a postcard to a friend from Paris: "Dinners, soirees, erratic millionaires, painters, translations, lobsters, absinthe, music, promenades, oysters, sapphic heiresses, editors, books . . . *And how!*" It must have been a little like that, too, in the 1960s.

Jim, in collaboration with Romain Gary, wrote much of the script of Darryl Zanuck's movie of the Normandy invasion, *The Longest Day*, and with the money from that bought the house on the Île, just down the way from the quarters where Ford Madox Ford had once edited *Transatlantic Review*. Their house was an old building put up in the early eighteenth century, as Jim once wrote, "by some long-vanished entrepreneur who was a big wheel in the King's Finance Ministry or someplace like that." They bought the house piecemeal, one floor at a time. Eventually it rambled over three stories of one building and extended into another floor of the house next door. The furnishings included a refectory table, many old straight-backed chairs and overstuffed sofas, Greek and Roman sculptures, Beauford Delaney paintings hanging slightly askew on the walls, a panoply of ancient arms here

and there, and an extensive library including numerous first
editions of American novels and poems and an outstanding
collection of books on the Civil War. The first floor included a
bedroom which had a denlike quality—a big round bed covered in fur and pillows, dark heavy curtains and French period furniture; and then a tiled bathroom with leopard skin on
the walls, and a small Japanese bridge going right over the
bathtub into a crawl-space which had mirrors and more leopard skin on the walls and ceiling. A winding staircase which
Jim had designed led upstairs to other eclectic rooms—each
with a good drawing fireplace—including a large room dominated by the ancient pulpit which served as the bar. Certain
dedicated Catholics, though known as hard drinkers, had
walked out of the house after seeing this bar. Because of the
bar, and the freewheeling nature of the parties, the American
business executives and their wives who might have been
brought by mutual friends usually did not return a second
time.

In his novel *The Merry Month of May,* he would make the
bar the property of his character Harry Gallagher, but it was
really *his* bar that he was writing about:

"Was there ever such a bar existed anywhere, in such an
apartment?"

> I guess Harry's bar needs a whole paragraph to it-
> self. It got to be famous in Paris. It was a wooden
> Renaissance pulpit, made over. What the French call
> a *chaire*, one of those pulpits which hang up on a
> column in the church, with a circular staircase
> mounting to it. In Harry's apartment it stood on the
> floor. He had hunted two years for it to find it. It cost
> him a lot; and it cost him almost as much to have his
> *ébéniste* fix it up for him. The *ébéniste* repaired it,

gave it a new, raised floor of ancient wood, and fitted it with two bar shelves of the same, for bottles. It was a five-sided object, with one side open at the back for the drink server (or priest) to enter. The other four sides were of wood panels, with peaked arches carved across their tops, below which dim worn figures carved in very low relief and vague with age could be presumed to be doing something religious. It jutted out from the far end wall of the room like the nose of a PT boat cresting a wave . . .

As if all this were not sacrilegious enough to suit him, or perhaps one could even say funny enough, humorous enough, Harry had completed the whole tableau with a clutch of five bar stools which were not bar stools at all but in reality those hardest to find and most expensive for their size Louis Treize items of all: the prie-Dieu prayer stools. There is a story that the first time Buñuel ever came to the place, he peered at Harry's bar and its accouterments and then seized the two-handed German sword and tried to cleave Harry from shoulder to waist as he carried a tray of glasses in from the kitchen, crying, "You son of a bitch! You son of a bitch! My mother used to pray on a prayer stool just like that!" And rushed from the house. Later, of course, he sent an apology.

There was a tradition in the house that anyone unable to make himself heard in one of the frequent political or literary arguments could announce, "I invoke the pulpit!" He then had the right to stand at the pulpit-bar and speak uninterrupted for three minutes. This right was only occasionally invoked and the no-interruption rule never enforced.

The countless people who came there would testify to the

timeless feeling of that house. It may have had the most spectacular view in all of Paris. It was right on top of the Seine, and the first thing one could see out of the enormous French windows or from the balcony was the nave of Notre Dame, and then the river flowing twenty feet below, with its boats and barges—and then the traffic on the street, and the people walking along the quai. Always there was music flowing out—Bach, perhaps, or Mozart, or Gershwin. As one visitor would recall years later, "There was a feeling of the goodness of life as mirrored in this singular vista, of fellowship and tranquillity and all the fine things that make life worth living."

In *The Merry Month of May,* Jim would write:

> . . . the back of Notre Dame with its soaring buttresses almost close enough to touch; the high wedding cake of the Pantheon on its hilltop floating above the old Left Bank houses; and always the river, and the barges, a never-ceasing source of interest to the eyeball. I had had my writing desk placed right in front of one of these windows. And down below were the old trees, and the ancient cobbled ramp, framed in ancient white stone, where the poor people from the tenements in the center of the Island used on Sundays to run their cars and motorbikes down to the water to wash them. It was a great place to live back in fifty-eight, when I first got it.

He did his work on the fourth floor of the house next door on the Île. He rose early, and got to work fairly early, even if it had been a late night. He worked slowly—a thousand words a day at the most, usually less. The room was filled with many of his acquisitions. Once Clem Wood went up there and found him teaching the lover of the maid how to load powder into cartridges. Many days he worked far past his usual quitting time of two-thirty or three. By six o'clock, the vanguard of his horde of thirsty friends would have begun to arrive.

Rose Styron remembers:

> I always seemed to be standing on that balcony with them, with the French doors thrown open behind us looking out on the river. They talked to everybody on the street. People would come by and wave to them and shout something up—people they didn't know, people they did. You'd see John Frankenheimer walking past and go up to his apartment for a drink, or down to Blair Fuller's ex-wife's place, or Eugene Braun-Munk's. Year after year when you went there, things would change, the kids would go away, something new was happening, but the balcony was always our focus. The trees were in bloom or they weren't, the lovers were leaning over the Seine or they weren't, it would be cold and rainy and you couldn't go out, then the sky would change and you'd see the spire and hear the bells, and the taxis would always be tooting away out there. I'd be up very early in the morning and so would Jim. We'd have breakfast and stand out on the balcony for a while and look at the day. Then he'd go upstairs to work and I'd go out and stroll across the bridge and look back up at the Jones place. It was Paris, that's what it was.

There had, of course, been a handful of prominent American salons in Paris over the years. In the twenties there was Gertrude Stein on the Rue de Fleurus and Natalie Barney on the Rue Jacob. The main place where writers mingled then was Shakespeare and Company, Sylvia Beach's English-language bookstore on the Left Bank, which was the center of the expatriate American colony. Equally so in the sixties and early seventies was the Jones house. It was a common ground for the peregrinating Americans of the day, helping them to know who they were, and where they had come from. The Sunday night spaghettis there became a Paris institution. Shortly after they moved to the Île, Gloria got pregnant and because of complications the doctor said she had to stay in bed the last four months. Since she had to remain very flat, she would more or less hold court on the telephone there. People would arrive in Paris from America and not know where to get things. They were advised to call Gloria. She would tell them which florist was good, or which butcher, or how best to find an apartment. Then friends would come around and cook. Their salon, if one must use that word, started that way.

"This was the place," Irwin Shaw remembers, "where the lonely could find friends, where the gregarious could converse, the literary could discuss theirs or anybody else's work, where love affairs could be arranged and the pain of broken marriages assuaged. Jim would seem to be a little bemused at what was happening in his house, but for the most part he enjoyed watching it all, and being a gracious host." These parties attracted just about every American living in or passing through Paris:

> . . . writers, painters, congressmen, racing stable owners, newspapermen, poker players, students, ambassadors, pregnant children in need of advice, editors with a predatory look in their eye, movie producers and directors, ambassadors, people hoping for a loan, theatrical ladies, avowed revolutionaries, and

assorted representatives of many professions, including the handsome doctor who took care of all American ills in Paris, worried about our livers, and had to change his telephone number because Elizabeth Taylor or Richard Burton would call him so often in the middle of the night at the first twinge of a headache.

"Every time a writer came to Paris," Irving "Swifty" Lazar, Jim's agent, said, "some Arab kid on the street would tell him, 'Be sure to go to the Joneses.' There's booze, and poker, and if you're lucky, you'll meet a pretty girl."

Eunice and Sargent Shriver were there frequently when he was the American ambassador; once Chief Justice Warren and his wife came by. Mary McCarthy was a close friend who was often there, as were the American movie people who had come to Paris after the witch-hunting years. Another good friend was James Baldwin, who would get drunk and stand behind the pulpit-bar and show everybody how he used to preach, and give a hellfire sermon on the evils of drink. William Burroughs, pale and skeletonal from his drug withdrawal and known by the Tangier street hustlers as *el hombre invisible*, was a welcomed guest, and so were the beat poets, Allen Ginsberg and Gregory Corso, when they roared through town. Samuel Beckett, James T. Farrell, Kenneth Tynan, Louis Malle, John Frankenheimer, Frank and Eleanor Perry, Gore Vidal, Jerzy Kosinski, Seymour Krim, Pat Lawford, Abraham Ribicoff, Art and Ann Buchwald, Enid Hardwicke, Arthur Miller, Thornton Wilder, Cyrus Sulzberger, Deborah Kerr, Peter Viertel, Nelson Algren, Bernard Malamud, Tennessee Williams, Lauren Bacall, Gene Kelly, Jean Seberg, and Kevin McCarthy were among the visitors. Elizabeth Weicker lived a few doors away on the Île, as did Claude

Dauphin. Sylvia Beach, who was quite old (she had stayed in Paris even through the Nazi occupation, and had been interned in an enemy alien camp), used to drop in all the time; so did Alice B. Toklas, Henry Miller and his Japanese wife, Man Ray and his wife, Alexander Calder, and Max Ernst—a blend of the twenties and the sixties. Once, at a party for Betty Comden and Adolph Green, who were over for a visit, François Truffaut led the Frenchmen there in "Singing in the Rain." A group of pro football players once arrived in the city to play a benefit football game for charity. The American lady in charge telephoned Gloria and said, "I didn't know all football players were black. What do you do with black football players?" So they came shortly to the house on the Île. "Which is the mean one?" Gloria asked, and Mean Joe Greene of the Pittsburgh Steelers said, "That's me, madame."

There was nothing very Parisian about these evenings, and sometimes people would have to go look out the windows at the quai and the Seine to remind themselves where they were.

One day a Japanese novelist named Ono who had fought against Jim as a young infantryman on Guadalcanal looked him up through his French publisher. He and his beautiful Japanese girlfriend—a liberated kind of girl—dropped by the house on the Île for a drink. They eventually stayed all night and ended up having breakfast in Les Halles at sunrise. It was a wonderful and touching night. The Japanese novelist and Jim talked for hours. They discussed which side had been more cruel, out there in the jungles of the 'Canal. They laughed and cried a lot, and after quite a few drinks began demonstrating their differing techniques on a battle charge. The Japanese showed off some of the karate they had taught him; Jim told him any good punch in the mouth was better.

117

The next day the Japanese girlfriend returned in ceremonial dress to give the Jones children some toys.

The place was also a magnet, as Bill Styron would recall, for "the most remarkable group of American no-counts, bums, and hustlers, who would simply turn up on the doorstep. Jim was unfailingly decent to them, and so of course was Gloria. But there was a line that one did not cross. Gloria ultimately became pretty good at an insult when it was called for."

> A horrid little radical French intellectual latched onto me at the time *The Confessions of Nat Turner* was being published in Paris. He'd gotten the message that I'd written a kind of fascist book. He had on one of those wide, ill-tailored French pin-striped suits and a pongee shirt. He kept saying how could a white man write this fascist treatment of black people. I looked over and Gloria was getting more and more indignant. It was building up in her. She kept making little growls in French. He didn't take the hint, but went on, "As Aptheker said . . ." She looked at him finally and said, "Hey, I bet you suck cocks." He asked, "What did you say?" "I said, I bet you suck cocks, don't you?" "No one ever said anything like that to me," he said. He was out of the house in two seconds.

The weekly poker games also became a fixture, many of them lasting far into the night. "Often there was over five hundred dollars in the pot," Clem Wood recalled. "Jim was a terror, scowling from under his green eyeshade. He employed intimidation techniques. Frequently he tried to buy the pot. I considered Gloria a better player. In fact, she was the best woman player I'd ever seen, the best sport, the most fun to play with, whether for peanuts or big money." The regulars included Monique Gonthier, Sydney Chaplin, Irwin Shaw, Bernie Frizell of CBS, Bodil Nielsen, Françoise Sagan, the painters Don Fink and Paul Jenkins, the French writer Eve Berger, and Edward Muniche, a Mauritanian poet who was always getting totally cleaned out. If Jim got on a losing streak, he would put on his ten-gallon $300 stetson to change his luck.

He was "a compulsive competitor," Clem Wood remembers:

> I never sat across a chessboard or a poker table from a grimmer, a *scarier* opponent. Even in athletics, which in the years when I knew him were supposed to be medically forbidden to him, he *had* to compete. I saw him throw out his knee running to first in a ball game with the kids; another time he did the same thing while shotputting in a Jones-Wood track meet. One day we had a game of touch football with the children in our garden in Paris. Too tame for Jim: He insisted on tackling. He made one successful line buck and ran for a touchdown in the rhododendrons, but on the next play got tackled by Maxine Grofsky (a real gutsy player, said to be the original of the girl in *Goodbye, Columbus*) and limped for weeks.

"He lived extravagantly and his time in Paris was a fifteen-year fete," Irwin Shaw remembers. "His liquor bills alone were shocking, but he was constantly worried about money. He was haunted by the fear of poverty and lived on a lordly scale." From time to time he did work on other movie scripts, and on some of them he would not allow his name in the credits. In 1965 he left Burroughs Mitchell and Scribner's and signed a three-book contract with Delacorte, at that time one of the largest contracts in publishing history.

When Darryl Zanuck was preparing to film *The Longest Day*, portions of which were from Jim and Romain Gary's script of the American scenes, he telegrammed Jim in Split, Yugoslavia, where the Joneses were briefly on vacation. Zanuck's urgent wire solicited Jim to correct a small piece of American dialogue. Jim wired back, "How much for it?" and Zanuck replied, "Fifteen thousand dollars." "Okay, shoot," was the response. The wire with the line of dialogue came from Zanuck: "I can't eat that bloody old box of *tunny* fish." Jim and Gloria sat on a rock on the beach and corrected the line to read: "I can't stand this damned old tuna fish."

Always there was the unstinting generosity. Kurt Vonnegut once found himself temporarily short of money in Paris with a $200 hotel bill to pay. He did not know a soul in the city, but then he thought of his fellow writer Jones, whom he had never met. He got his number from the book and telephoned him, and Jim was at the hotel in fifteen minutes with the money. Jim had so much money, Vonnegut recalled, because it was Saturday, and he needed it for that night's poker game. He invited Vonnegut to play and told him the most anyone could lose would be $200. Vonnegut arrived at midnight, and Jim himself was down by $600.

He and Romain Gary were known as the two easiest touches in Paris. During particularly hard days in South Africa, a black South African refugee telephoned and said he had a letter of introduction. Gloria knew he was coming over. She was in the bathtub and heard the ring at the door. By the time she had· put on a robe and come out, Jim had already given the refugee six hundred dollars.

With Gloria on the quai in Paris, 1959.
(*Gloria Jones Collection*)

With Gloria and Kaylie aboard the S.S. *France*, 1962, shortly
after he had finished *The Thin Red Line*.
(Gloria Jones Collection)

Jamie Jones at age five, photographed by his father.
(Gloria Jones Collection)

1960. From left to right: James Jones; Sylvia Beach
(who published James Joyce and ran the Shakespeare Press
in Paris); Thornton Wilder; and Alice B. Toklas.
(*Photo by Centre Culturel Américain*)

With William Styron at Biarritz in 1965.
(*Gloria Jones Collection*)

Poker at the Joneses' house in Paris. From left to right:
Bernie Frizell, the artist Addie Herder, and James Jones
during the course of a very serious game, 1967.
(Loomis Dean, Life Magazine, © 1967, Time Inc.)

The Joneses at their favorite brasserie on the Île St. Louis,
with Lady Susan and Sir Anthony Glyn, 1967.
(Loomis Dean, Life Magazine, © 1967, Time Inc.)

Jim, Gloria, Kaylie, and Jamie walking up from the Seine, 1967.
(Gloria Jones Collection)

In Sagaponack, 1974, when he was hard at work on *Whistle*.
(Photo by David Morris)

In Vietnam, 1973.
(Gloria Jones Collection)

I used to holler a lot about Jim giving away money, so he looked at me guiltily. Then he phoned Romain Gary and said, "There's a young man here from South Africa," and Romain said, "Jim, I'm busy. How much?" And Jim said, "I'll split it with you halfies. Your part's three hundred dollars." Romain said, "Okay, I'll send it right over."

Muriel Murphy was there in 1968 on the way to the Vaucluse and, although she did not know him well then, asked him where she could get an English keyboard typewriter, which were not on sale anywhere in Paris, to take with her. He loaned her the old, battered portable on which he had written *From Here to Eternity*, and he warned her that whenever she used the F key in her letters home, the typewriter would automatically print *Fuck*.

Joseph Heller remembers that in 1961, when *Catch-22* was about to be published, "one day a telegram came from Paris and it was from James Jones saying he loved the book. So did Irwin Shaw and Art Buchwald. I was astonished, because both Jones and Shaw had written war novels, and I thought there would be a certain amount of jealousy. But there wasn't, and my publisher even redesigned the book jacket to include their quotes."

The many homeless, wandering young Americans who found themselves at the house on the Île in these years would remember his characteristic kindness and warmth. Bill Belli, later to become a prosperous attorney, was one of them. He was traveling around Europe, almost broke and without much purpose, trying, he said, to find out who he was. William Burroughs brought him to a small dinner at the Jones house. "I was ill at ease and terribly unsure of myself. I hardly said a word. When the other people were leaving, Jim took me aside and said, 'Hang around for a drink.' I think he'd sensed my discomfort, almost as if I'd reminded him of something in himself a long time ago. I stayed and we had a good long talk."

"When I lunched or walked with him on the Island," Clem Wood remembered, "I was struck by the number of people in the street, in the *tabac* or the *épiceries*, who would call out, 'Bonjour, Monsieur Jones. Ça va?' Jim would growl 'Ça va' and walked on. He was known, respected, and loved in his quarter of the city."

Better than most, the boy from the Wabash Valley knew his way around Paris. He knew, for instance, precisely where to find the best straight razors in the city. He would be walking around with a friend from America and on a whim take him up a narrow street to some tiny shop on the Left Bank near the Université. They would climb three flights of stairs and there would be a little wisp of a man waiting to show them the finest straight razors in the world. He was always finding people like that: dealers in pornography, or in Pakistani jewelry, or in old chess sets. He knew the little art galleries, the antique shops, the stores that carried Army memorabilia, the places to browse among dusty bric-a-brac.

So too with the bars and restaurants. They would frequent the likely ones—meeting people at the Deux Magots or the Café Flore in the fading sunlight and watching the world go by before proceeding to dinner; Chez Castel in St. Germain des Prés, which was somewhat like what Elaine's in New York would be; the Village across the boulevard from the Deux Magots, where the French and Americans mingled and where

Jim and Gloria became friendly with the French writers who favored Algerian independence; La Coupole in Montmartre which they would stroll to with the first touch of spring; or the Brasserie Lipp in St. Germain, with its revolving-door entrance, for good talk with Romain Gary or Irwin Shaw or Mary McCarthy and lunches of Alsatian food, sauerkraut, *cassoulet* served in earthenware casseroles, and Belon oysters, sometimes $40 or $50 worth of oysters at one sitting, and the big schooners of beer which were called *un sérieux* at Lipp.

If there were "a state lunch" involving publishers, Eugene Braun-Munk recalled, "Jim's eyes would light up and he'd say, 'Can we stick 'em for Garin?'" and they would go to that big, expensive restaurant off Place Makert and have truffles, roast beef, and three different wines and discuss the publicity of a new book of his that might be coming out in France or Germany.

At Lipp he became a special client among its literary and film-world clienteles, part of a tradition going back to Fitzgerald, Hemingway, Edith Wharton, and Cocteau in the twenties, and much before that. He got celebrity treatment there. If anyone failed to recognize *le grand écrivain* Zhemz Zhawnz, Gloria would enlighten him: "This is my husband, the great writer." In *The Merry Month of May* he described this singular meeting place:

> The waiters always dressed in black tuxedo-like suits and aprons and black bow ties from an earlier day. They all wore numbered metal checks on their lapels which signified strictly their proper place in the waiter hierarchy, and their seniority was a very jealously guarded thing . . .
> The rest of the place was like its waiters. By step-

ping through the door you might have stepped back
into the year 1900. There were no tables in the center
of the floor in the back, only a big serving cabinet,
which held the napkins and the bread and condi-
ments and silverware: *les couverts*. The waiters continually clustered around it to get their serving stuff.
The electric light fixtures looked like they should be
gaslights. Each wall was decorated with a three-foot
mirror above the seatbacks, and if you craned your
neck you could see the lights and the mirror and the
people reflected and re-reflected almost to an infinity.
Between the lengths of mirror were murals made of
tiny highly colored tiles which represented plants.
The front was almost exactly like the back except
that it was wider and a waist-high wood partition
ran down the center making it two rooms. One side
was for coffee and drinking only. The other side was
for eating. Along its top was a slightly raised plate of
glass, so that people could talk under it to each other
and see who all was there. Upstairs on the first floor
was still another salle, but nobody went there except
the unknowns.

Or there were undiscovered, out-of-the-way places like the
Vietnamese ones which Jim would search out all over Paris—
some of the best food in the world—or the little Alsatian brasserie on the Île where they would meet friends at two-thirty in
the afternoon after he had finished work. He was adept with
the wine, and became something of a gourmet without being
an idiot about it all—a merging of the American palate, which
is said to be honest, with the sophistication of the French. At
the brasserie on the Île he would introduce visitors from back
home to a dish called *museau*. The French were noted for

thousand-foot drop. Jim caught him by the shirt and held onto him, Triz's life hanging there in the balance. "It was like an awful rescue movie, a nightmare," Triz remembered. "There were just the three of us. Jim held onto me for a long time on that goddamned cliff, grasping my shirt with one arm. Gloria reached for me too. But Jim saved my life. He gradually pulled me up. It took an incredible strength." Kay Kendall, who soon afterward died of cancer and whom they all loved for her humor, fun, and laughter, became ill that summer and needed vitamin injections. Except for the Italian doctors down in the village, Jim from his Army days was the only one around who knew how to administer shots. Then, Gloria and Triz remember, Jim himself had a sudden, strange attack, a precursor perhaps of what might have become his fatal illness. He choked and got blue in the face; he was thirty-nine years old. The Italian doctors said he had merely choked on coffee and prescribed vitamin B shots. For the rest of that summer of '59 in Portofino Jim and Kay Kendall had a ritual once a day: letting down their bikinis and giving each other vitamin shots.

Triz remembered that the only time he ever saw Jim actually ready for physical violence was one night that summer. Jim was doing a lot of scuba diving with two fellows—one who had been an enlisted man in the Italian Army during the war as an underwater demolition expert, the other a rather simple Italian man who had a small boat. They invited the two men to the castle for dinner. In the village that day Gloria had run into Jackie Rogers, a model in Paris, who was with an Italian prince, and asked them to dinner too. Throughout dinner the prince was rude and disdainful to the two common Italians; when he talked to them at all, he talked down to them. "Jim was fuming," Triz recalled. "I'd never seen him so angry. 'If he keeps this up,' he said to me, 'I'm going to throw that fuckin' dandy off the mountain.'" So Triz took Jackie Rogers aside and told her she had better get the prince out of there quick, and she did so.

In Paris the good life was weekend outings on the Seine and the Marne, gangs of their friends and various children in different rowboats ending up at twilight in some little restaurant in the countryside; swinging parties at the Dutch, Israeli, or American embassies; visits to the all-night White Russian cabarets—where all the talent was over fifty years old, Irwin Shaw remembered, and the Russian exiles played guitars, danced Gypsy dances, sang sorrowful winter songs, and drank to your health and the czar's with your own champagne.

Jim and Gloria were friendly with many of the black Americans in the city, and there were evenings with Richard Wright and his wife in the soul-food place in Montmartre where the black musicians would hang out. Since Jim had an idea of writing a book on Django Reinhardt, they got to know all the jazz people very well. These were the last great days of Lester Young, Hazel Scott, and Kenny Clarke, and Billie Holiday was singing at a place called The Blue Note on the Right Bank off the Champs Elysées, a comedown from her glory years. Between acts one evening she was sitting at the bar next to the Joneses and turned to them and said, "May I please have a drink?" Since the proprietors had warned them never to buy her a drink, they ignored her. She said it again: "May I have a drink, *please?*" and again they did not respond. Finally, she put her face next to Jim's and shouted: *"Hey, asshole, get me a drink!"* He bent over laughing, and against all advice got her something immediately, and they had a long evening talking.

Beauford Delaney, the black expatriate painter from Nashville, was among the many people he helped. Jim and Gloria would go out to his studio in Clarmart to eat stew and drink wine; one night they were accompanied by Tennessee Williams. Delaney, a compulsive walker, used to walk miles across Paris to visit the house on the Île. When Delaney grew older and became ill, Jim helped him with large commissions and wrote many of the blurbs and descriptions of his paintings for the art catalogues.

It is best to have Bill Styron's words on what he calls "the monumental drunk of 1960":

> It was my last night in Europe after a long trip—the night before we were to sail on the *United States* from Le Havre. Jim and I decided to get good and drunk, no fooling around. Jimmy Baldwin was with us. We had a few drinks before dinner, then a really fine meal, and we went out. Rose and Gloria dropped out around midnight. We were in some nightclubs, and some girls still clung around for a while. Finally even Jimmy Baldwin faded—a very good man with the bottle. He folded around four or five A.M., to give him credit maybe a little longer. The collapse of Jimmy Baldwin should've given us pause for thought, but didn't. Dawn was coming up, a beautiful late summer's morning. Jim and I decided to carry on. So we opened a little brasserie on the Left Bank and talked about life, love, literature, mortality, and sex. My wife and kids and I had to leave Paris at 7 P.M. to drive to Le Havre. All the more reason to stay up.

At twelve noon promptly Jim and I were drinking straight-up martinis at the Ritz Bar, not an eye's-wink of sleep. We were still standing up boozing until three in the afternoon. By this time it was beginning to wear on us a little, eighteen hours straight. We poured ourselves into a taxi and went back to the Ile, with this bizarre feeling of going home drunk in the middle of the afternoon. We went in the house and the first thing I heard was a huge crash. Gloria had hurled a big teapot at both of us which missed Jim's head by an inch and shattered against the wall. Then this scream: "If I ever lay eyes on you again may God kill me, you drunken bum!" I retired discreetly to the front room, gathered my family, bade a messy goodbye, and left for America.

The Jones family were by no means troublemaking. Jim Jones was one of the hardest workers around—a life of diligent application—and for days on end he would not leave the house. For that matter, the American community in Paris in the 1960s was considerably less raucous than its counterpart in the 1920s, when people like E. E. Cummings and Hart Crane were forever getting embroiled with the gendarmes. But this is not to say, also, that there were not troubles of a kind that writers and writers' wives in the nature of things are destined to get into every now and again.

On Christmas Eve of 1959, while in the company of celebrating friends, Jim Jones ran his white Mercedes convertible into a statue of a French hero and broke some ribs and lost some teeth. After his arrest, the Paris police interviewed him closely and allowed him to telephone his wife, then locked him in a cell. The police went over the transcript of their interview in Gloria's presence and were mystified by such expressions as "monkey-fuckers" and "ape-shitters." Despite this, he got off with a stiff fine and the loss of his driver's license for a while.

Their friend Addie Herder, the artist who lived in Paris in these years, would remember an altercation or two. "Here I was a nice Jewish girl in a funny bar with my friends the Joneses and all hell broke loose. It wasn't even our fault." They were in a private club called the Rive Gauche. Some spoiled rich children of Americans who had been creative in the twenties were there. "They wanted to talk with us, and we didn't feel like talking with them, that was all, and one of them threw a bottle at us. Jim was on crutches from a broken leg that he got skiing and wasn't involved. Gloria and I started swinging, however." A general brawl ensued. All the French in the place came over to watch. *"Les américaines!"* one of them shouted. "They're just like they are in the movies!" Then the French got in the fight, and everybody started hitting everybody else, until a truce finally settled in.

Their children Jamie and Kaylie were enrolled in a private Protestant school on St. Germain. The teacher sent word home that Jamie, then seven years old, was being punished for some minor infraction. Jamie's mother went to the school to confer with the teacher; she asked where her son was. The teacher replied that he was locked up in the *vestiaire*. Gloria, not quite sure of the language, took *vestiaire* to mean "closet," rather than "cloakroom." "Fuck you—you won't lock my son in a closet!" she shouted, and hit the teacher with an uppercut, for which both children were expelled from school.

One night in the white Mercedes convertible, while driving down the Boulevard St. Germain, Jim and Gloria had a marital spat. He lost his temper, stopped the car, got out, and walked away, slamming the door so hard that the window broke. The glass sprayed all over the street. A gendarme came to investigate; crowds gathered, as they will in France. "Qu'est-ce qui se passe?" the gendarme asked. "Mon mari est en colère," Gloria wanted to reply, which means "very angry," but instead it came out sounding *en chaleur,* which means "very hot sexually." The gendarme said in French: "Go home, madame. You're very lucky."

There were also tricks. Their friend Jean Castel owned a popular bar and restaurant down a side street in St. Germain. For a long time this establishment and its owner had been terrorized by an old Romanian woman, who stood outside in a dirty flowing dress playing a squeaky mandolin, occasionally shouting obscenities through the doorway at Mr. Castel inside. Castel complained about this woman to anyone who would listen. She was ruining his business and her damnable music was driving him insane, he said, but what could he do? There were even rumors of a lawsuit. Castel announced to his friends that he was going to take a much-needed vacation in Tahiti—a long plane ride indeed from Paris. About twenty-five of his friends, led by the Joneses, put up $100 apiece and bought the Romanian woman a round-trip ticket to Tahiti the day before Castel was to leave Paris. He took his plane, and many hours later landed at the airport in Tahiti. He descended the ramp, and almost collapsed at the sight which greeted him: the Romanian woman strumming her mandolin and saying: "Welcome to Tahiti, Monsieur Castel."

Over the years the Joneses had a menagerie of servants: Judith, the Portuguese who was with them for fifteen years; Judith's mother; the Brazilian homosexual cook Carlos; and the French-Algerian maid Marlene and Marlene's lover.

"No one in all of Europe lived a more *complicated* life than the Joneses," their friend Clem Wood recalled. He tells this story about the maid Marlene and the cook Carlos:

Marlene, who used to work for us, approached my wife Jessie one day at the Joneses' and told her she was very upset because Gloria suspected her of borrowing her dresses. Now, Marlene was scarcely five feet tall; it was obvious that the cook Carlos was wearing Gloria's clothes on his day out. Jessie advised Marlene to keep quiet and let Gloria make this discovery for herself. Some time later, my stepson Jamie Bruce told me that he, Jamie Jones, and Kaylie had seen Carlos getting out of a taxi wearing a white evening gown, and that Kaylie had called out: "Hey, Carlos, what are you doing in my mother's dress?" (Jamie's comment to me was: "Really, can you imagine asking such a rude question?") The Carlos affair came to a head when Jim and Gloria rented a house near us in Spetsai. They moved in with Carlos, the kids, and the three cats. Carlos soon became notorious on the island. He used to send his wigs to the local beauty parlor every day. No one in Greece had ever seen a black Brazilian drag queen before. By the end of a month, the Joneses had decided he had to go. But there was a problem: Jim, Gloria, and the children were going directly from Greece to Spain, while Carlos was supposed to fly back to Paris with the cats. They decided to fire him by writing. Since neither Jim nor Gloria could write in French, the dismissal note was written by Kaylie and Jamie Bruce, both about twelve, and handed to Carlos as he stepped on the boat for Athens. Then Gloria had misgivings: "Jesus, Clem, you don't think he'll just say 'Fuck it' and dump the cats overboard?" The cats arrived safely.

His Americanness never left him. When John Kennedy was shot, he wandered around Paris in a daze, going to places where he knew Americans would be—"searching out Americans, and finding them, in all the American-frequented bars, where we all sort of just stood together like wet birds buying each other drinks and nodding our heads and saying almost nothing." There is an autobiographical passage in *The Merry Month of May* about his thoughts on the death of Bobby Kennedy, recalling him on a visit to the Styrons:

> Sitting with the newspaper in my apartment, I remembered one night at a lawn party in Martha's Vineyard where I was visiting, when some of the Kennedy clan had whipped over in their boat from the Cape, and when after all the shouted hellos and laughter and drinks and the barbecue itself, I saw him sitting by himself on the old porch rail, a porch rail which came right out of another time. He had one foot in its expensive loafer up on the rail and was clasping his knee and looking out over the lawn and smiling, all alone, enjoying the moonlight and the party. There were lots of children squealing and playing on the dark lawn, and there was a local band of sorts playing a modified rock. Kennedy simply sat, smiling, enjoying, his blond shock of longer hair hanging down over his forehead.

One afternoon Jim and Gloria were walking along the Champs Elysées when he sighted Joe Louis, strolling down the sidewalk alone in an orange jacket with his name written on it. He went up to Joe Louis, extended his hand, and said, "Mr. Louis, I'm one of your greatest admirers." He kept pumping Louis' hand in front of a gathering crowd of Frenchmen and telling him what a great man he was.

He enjoyed what happened to him one day at a movie set. Paul Newman and John Frankenheimer had invited him to come out and watch the filming of a movie they were doing. A worker on the set saw him and came up and said: "Hey, I know you. Did you ever write that story you were always talking about?"

"Yeah."

"What did you call it?"

"From Here to Eternity."

This flustered the man. The two of them had had a job together in the late 1940s, moving trailers around in trailer parks in Tennessee and Kentucky.

Once he wrote an essay in an art catalogue for another of his many painter friends living in Paris, Alice Baber. She was from the village of Kansas, Illinois, twenty miles south of Robinson, and a direct descendant of Lincoln's mother, Nancy Hanks. He was remembering his own Midwest:

> One can see and feel an almost terrifying poignancy, a near weeping sadness and sorrow in these delicately gay and summer-bright colors. It is as if she is trying to tell us about her native Illinois, with its brilliant blinding sun, its dust, its summer-deep greens, that summer itself will not stay. School must begin again, grandmothers and old people will not last the winter. One feels a strange choking sorrow over the gay beauty she shows us.

Despite the sophistication which surrounded him, the way he talked—the grammar, the border-state drawl—remained essential to this Americanness. Surely those Americans who spurn their native talk are really spurning their deepest origins. He talked the way he grew up, and as he did in the Army. He spoke as his characters spoke.

He wanted his children to have the flavor of America, and he encouraged this in curious ways. On Sunday afternoons American Westerns, dubbed in French, were shown on Paris television. Almost every Sunday he and his son Jamie would dress in cowboy suits and watch these Westerns. Jim would shout back things at the TV set. "Don't ask for the fuckin' *vin rouge*—say *redeye,* you assholes!" Sometimes for the children he would imitate the way Deputy Dawg walked in the cartoons. The children, apparently, thought this behavior perfectly normal. They did not know for years that every American father did not do this kind of thing.

One Sunday afternoon Rose Styron arrived at the house straight from the airport and rang the bell two or three times, then pushed the bell next door where the maid Judith lived. "Oh yes," she said, "Monsieur Jones and Jamie are in the bedroom downstairs. It's soundproof and they can't hear you." Judith led her downstairs.

> There the two of them were. They still hadn't heard me. They were sitting on the edge of the round fur-covered bed in full American cowboy outfits, both of them, with matching hats and boots, holsters, the works. They were two feet from the television set in which James Cagney was dancing "Yankee Doodle Dandy." They were singing along with it. They were so engrossed they didn't see me for a long time.

The war, like America, was never very far away, as if it were the thread to his life, holding together all the fragmentary parts of it—as indeed in large measure it was. He went often to the battlefields of World War I and II. Once he and Gloria took a week and visited the World War I battlefields in the cold, ugly part of France. Almost every year around the sixth of June he made a pilgrimage to Normandy and tramped all over the D-day beaches and the disputed terrain inland until he got to know them intimately.

Utah was a long, lonely windswept beach that stretched for miles and miles, with one tiny little monument on it to mark the landings. The English beaches were relatively flat country, much of it through towns and built-up areas, with the large town of Ouistreham and its famous casino and the Orne estuary on the left flank . . . At Omaha I climbed up and sat awhile on the edge of the bluff, and looked down into the cup-shaped area with the sea at its back. It too had been built back up, and the six or eight tall spindly French summer homes have been rebuilt. It was easy to see what a murderous converging fire could be brought to bear on the beaches from the curving bluff. Especially to an old infantryman. And it was easy to half-close your eyes and imagine what it must have been like. The terror and total confusion, men screaming or sinking silently under the water, tanks sinking as their crews drowned inside, landing craft going up as a direct hit took them, or grating ashore to discharge their live cargo into the already scrambled mess, officers trying to get their men together, medics trying to find shelter for the wounded, until finally out of the welter a "certain desperate order began to emerge," and men began to move toward the two bottleneck exits. I sat there until my friends began to yell at me from down below, and I fervently thanked God or Whomever that I had not been there.

Once, while on a trip to Italy, he drove down from Rome to look at Anzio, which had been "one long hellish nightmare— in a pocked, surreal, destroyed, pest-inhabited landscape."

Today what used to be minefields is completely built over with seaside villas, restaurants, and bars. But it is easy for any old soldier to see the complete hellishness of the position, with the two towns, Anzio and Nettuno, dominated by the Alban hills, and no rear area at all beyond the harbor except the expanse of the open sea.

I went around to look at the American Military Cemetery afterward, which is placed off a few miles somewhere else. For a while I walked around among the crosses that formed the headstones, on the green, well-kept grass. The magnitude of all the long lines of white crosses was truly awesome. I talked to the man in charge, a red-bearded American who lived right there. No, not many people came, he said. It was too far away, and off the main tourist routes from Rome. And of course the local Italians had no reason to be there. But he liked to make sure the place was always well-kept, anyway. Sometimes it was hard, on the budget the U.S. government allot- ted him. But once in a while somebody might come by who had a relative buried there; or else someone like myself, who was just interested. I thanked him, and told him his caretaking was superb, which it was. What else was there to say? I got in my little car and drove back.

8.

In the years from 1966 to 1973 in Paris he wrote five books: *Go to the Widow-Maker, The Ice-Cream Headache and Other Stories, The Merry Month of May, A Touch of Danger,* and *Viet Journal.* All this time he was also working slowly on *Whistle,* and spending an occasional summer on Long Island.

The word was out in the New York publishing business in 1965 that he was leaving Scribner's, which had become quite conservative in its advances to authors, to sign a lucrative contract with Trident Press, known mainly as the publisher of Harold Robbins. Don Fine was editor in chief of Dell and had helped set up Delacorte Press in 1964. His superiors, having heard the rumor that Jim was leaving Scribner's, said to him: "Go get Jones."

Fine was from Battle Creek, Michigan, graduated from

Harvard in 1943, and went into Signal Corps intelligence in the Pacific. He was an admirer of Jim's work and believed *From Here to Eternity* to be the great novel to come out of the war. "I also hated officers. God, how I hated them. They were all dummies then. That's one of the reasons I thought Jones and I might get along." Fine telephoned Jim in Paris on an impulse and introduced himself. Jim refused to talk with him on the grounds that the Trident contract was ready to be signed; he was always a suspicious man about his deals anyway. So Fine took a plane to Paris the next day, checked into the George V, and telephoned Jim again at the house on the Île.

"Goddam, I already told you I can't talk to you," he said.

Fine was persistent, inviting him to lunch at the George V. "Well, okay, but I'm bringing my wife."

"He was the most sophisticated man I ever met," Fine remembered. "He had immediate insights into things that mattered. He understood things." Fine spent four days in Paris and stayed with the Joneses constantly. He promised to match the Trident contract, or go better.

"I don't even know you," Jim said.

"Well, try me. I've read everything you've written. Ask me anything about your work. Ask me about other writers."

They talked for a long time that day about literature. The visiting editor had just gotten out of a hospital in New York with ulcers and was unable to drink. "Good," Jim said. "I like an editor who don't drink." Because of his ulcers, Fine had brought a briefcase full of bottles of Margel antacid. He had to carry the briefcase with him everywhere and take a swig of the Margel every half hour, even in the most proper Parisian restaurants. The Joneses took him to several parties. "Gloria went around telling their friends that here was this New York editor who had come to Paris to sign up her husband and was carrying around a million dollars in his briefcase. Actually all I had in there was that damned Margel." Jim took a taste and liked it; later Fine sent him a private supply with his name on each bottle. The result of Fine's visit was that he signed his man for Delacorte to a three-book contract at $300,000 a book, plus company fringe benefits for the entire family.

Jim began work on his novel set in the Caribbean, *Go to the Widow-Maker*, and Fine had several working sessions with him in the summer of 1966 on Long Island. "We argued a lot. But he was good to work with—very comic and serious at the same time, one of the funniest men I ever knew. He'd read a passage and say, 'Don't you think this is funny?' I'd agree, then he'd say, 'Them dumb assholes won't think so. I can't put a notation on this saying, 'This is supposed to be funny.'"

Go to the Widow-Maker, published in 1967, was Delacorte's first best seller, reaching number nine for a while; it was a huge best seller in paperback. It said as well as anything he had written about the whole notion of manliness and what it really is, as opposed to what people think it is. He also wrote beautifully about women in this novel; his character Lucky was patterned on Gloria. Many of the descriptive passages—skin diving in Jamaica, life at the Olafson Hotel in Haiti—were marvelously vivid.

But the book was a critical disaster, inspiring perhaps the most vicious reviews of a single book by a serious American novelist in the whole generation. It suffered largely from a kind of willed quality—"not written from the inside like the other earlier books," one of the friendlier critics of it would later write. "Descriptive truth, not inner truth: a visitor's discovery." His later editor at Delacorte, Ross Claiborne, believed that much of the critical establishment, undeservedly so, turned against him after *Go to the Widow-Maker,* to the point that his next three books drew less attention on the book pages than anything he had ever written.

During the Paris revolution of 1968 the Joneses became close friends with Eugene Braun-Munk. Braun-Munk was a flamboyant figure, a large man in his early thirties, an intellectual who wore a monocle and unusual clothes. He had come to Paris as a book importer and distributor and eventually became Jim's main European editor. His ancestry was German-Hungarian, and he had been raised in New York by an uncle from Kentucky named Mac and his Hungarian wife Olga. When Braun-Munk met Jim, he told him the advice his Kentucky uncle Mac had given him before he went into the Army: "Now, you're going into the Army, and you watch out for them New York, Chicago guys. They won't do you no good. Hook up with a snake-hipped Southern boy who won't do you no harm."

During the revolution and after, the Joneses became his family. "We were overtaken by this big event which happened right in the heart of the city where we were living. All of the young people were exalted by what was happening." Since he was working in a large French firm and dealt with French colleagues and French problems, Jim looked to him to report and explain the daily events of the revolt, as well as to the children of their friends who were deeply involved. "They called me 'our European,'" he recalled. "It was all exactly as Jim described it in *The Merry Month of May.*" Braun-Munk was to be the character Hoffman-Beck in that novel.

"Even then he always talked of *Whistle,* the book he

141

wanted so to finish. He told me how difficult it was for him to go on with, to keep going."

During the days of the revolution Genta Hawkins, a young Foreign Service officer who had grown up in California, came to Paris to be a special assistant to Ambassador Sargent Shriver. She got to know the Joneses, as Braun-Munk had, in those hectic days of the student uprising, and like Braun-Munk became part of the family. Jim would introduce her as his "adopted daughter" and based the character Sweet Marie in *A Touch of Danger* on her.

> Jim delighted in your escapades, although it saddened him that he couldn't save or protect the people he loved from being hurt. He was always there, no matter how foolish you had been, never judging or condemning. He understood that you had to go through it on your own and in your own way.
>
> He was in his mellow years when I knew him. His rage at idiocy and injustice had become less belligerent and a more resigned indignation. But I had heard the stories of the wild years—the heavy drinking, the fights—and I was intimidated by them. I dreaded the thought of ever seeing the gentle man I knew transformed into some kind of hostile monster. He started drinking heavily again one summer in Deauville when he was finishing *The Merry Month of May*. The confrontation I had dreaded so took place when I was about to go off with the son of a close friend of Jim's. Jim called me aside and, holding my face in his hands, looked at me intensely and said, with his gruff voice cracking slightly, "I don't care how much you play around, but Jesus, I don't want you to get hurt." Some tough guy.

In 1967 Don Fine left Delacorte to form his own publishing company, and Ross Claiborne became Jim's editor. It was a working relationship that would span ten years. Claiborne had grown up outside Philadelphia, graduated from Lawrenceville, and went straight into the Army in 1944. He was sent through a speedy basic training and joined the 328th Infantry Division of the Third Army just as it was crossing the Rhine. He was wounded by a sniper's bullet, underwent a series of operations, and was on a hospital ship returning to the United States on the day the Japanese surrendered. By the fall of 1945 he was a freshman at Yale, where he studied English and creative writing. He helped found Delacorte in 1964 and eventually became its editorial director, working with such writers as Irwin Shaw, Kurt Vonnegut, William Goldman, and Jim Jones.

He began to see the Joneses in Paris in the late 1960s. Jim was talking with him about *Whistle* back then, although four books would come in between. Because he had been so deeply affected by the Paris revolts of 1968, he decided to write *The Merry Month of May* quite suddenly. Claiborne had a house on eastern Long Island, and grew to know Jim best when he took a place in East Hampton for part of the summer of 1969.

> Jim was a man who didn't form a friendship instantly. I think he was very wary of me. He and Don Fine had had a good relationship. Jim and I were so unalike. Finally we did become close—with *Whistle* —but he took a long time to make up his mind about people. I was totally in awe of the man and his reputation.

Jim was still drinking heavily in that period. He and Claiborne finished their work on *The Merry Month of May*, and Claiborne said they should celebrate. He made a reservation at a highly proper restaurant in Amagansett with a tearoom atmosphere, much crystal and bric-a-brac in a small dining room.

It couldn't have been a worse choice. Jim had started drinking at four or five in the afternoon. He and Monique Gonthier were behaving outrageously. Jim's voice reverberated through that small room till all the crystal rattled. By the time we'd been there five minutes the two owners were hovering around, practically pushing the check at me. Jim said at the top of his voice, "Monique, how do you say cocksucker in French?" I couldn't get out of there faster.

Claiborne recalled his early relationship with Gloria:

I've got to tell you, she scared the *hell* out of me when I first met her in Paris in the late sixties. Here I was a buttoned-down conservative type and she was this wild, beautiful, freewheeling dame who said everything that came into her mind. I was afraid we'd never get to be friends. But the more I saw of her, and saw them together, it was the best marriage I'd ever observed. They gave each other so much. Gloria in her totally honest way was precisely what Jim had to have, maybe the kind of woman that any writer like Jim Jones should have. With all the difficulties of being a star writer—his being so sniped at and taking his work so seriously and never telling you how deeply he was hurt—I admire how supportive and wonderful she was. She was terribly special and contributed to his life and well-being and work.

The Merry Month of May, published in 1971, was a fictional account of the Paris revolution, and the main characters are a group of American expatriates caught up in the passion and complexity of the student uprisings. Although the Book-of-the-Month Club took it as a main selection, it did not become a best seller; again, the response was largely critical.

In his inscription in the leather-bound copy of *The Merry Month of May* to his son Jamie on his eleventh birthday, he wrote:

> I wonder what you'll think of all this, and all of us
> when you're old enough to appreciate it all.
> I guess it doesn't matter.
> It's fun for me to do anyway. I get my kicks.
> God bless you, Jamie. I love you always.
>
> Dad

And to his daughter Kaylie: "You guys are moving too fast for me to keep up. I can't promise when the next one will be. Or even what. Maybe *Whistle.*"

Ross Claiborne began seeing the early chapters of *Whistle* during this time. When Jim sent him from Paris the first of the novel's five long sections, entitled "The Ship," with descriptions that matched Claiborne's own experiences on a hospital ship in 1945, he was profoundly moved. "*Whistle* to me was Jim Jones writing at his very best, which is as good as anyone. I sensed at once that it was truly going to be his masterpiece, the culminating experience of his life. I was disturbed that he kept putting it aside to do other things."

One of the things he did was a detective novel, *A Touch of Danger;* Doubleday made a much higher offer for it than Delacorte and published it in 1973. It is about an aging detective named Lobo and his contacts with the drug traffic and a group of violent expatriate hippies. The action is set on a Greek island several hours by boat from Athens, patterned after the island of Spetsai, where the Joneses' good friends Clem and Jessie Wood had a house. The Jones family visited there three summers. Clem Wood recalled that time:

> Jim loved this island, a fact you would hardly guess from reading *A Touch of Danger*. As a house guest present (and a damned expensive one), the Joneses hired a caïque that took us out every day to various coves and beaches around the island. Gloria stocked the boat with booze and hired Jessie's son Leigh as bartender. Cocktails began when we went aboard at 11 A.M. Gloria needed about four gin and tonics before she would swim. Jim gave all the kids scuba diving lessons. One year Gloria collected three beautiful black ladies, took them out every day, and taught them to swim. ("Spades can't swim because they won't let 'em in public pools.") The liquor bill alone for the caïque came to $600 for a month. The rest of the day and night was spent in games: chess, backgammon, poker. We had family chess tournaments, always won by Jim.
>
> The characters in *A Touch of Danger* are all very close to life, although the plot is of course invented. Lobo's landlady is the owner of the house Jim rented (right down to her "bad paintings"), and her husband is exactly like that lady's real husband, and her lover like her lover. I remember when I read the typescript of the book and pointed out to Jim that the woman on whom he had modeled a character he called "the baroness Chantal" was in fact a baroness. Reluctantly Jim wrote on the first page of the manu-

script: "Note to Printer: Change 'baroness' to 'count-ess' throughout."

When the book appeared, the husband of the real baroness, an Austrian gentleman of about seventy, came to me trembling with rage and said: "I shall have to challenge your friend Jones to a duel." "You can't do that," I said. "Jim has a very bad heart." "Ah," said the Austrian, greatly relieved.

Eugene Braun-Munk recalled an incident in this period. He and Jim went to Geneva as part of a publicity tour on *A Touch of Danger*. A blunder had been made in Braun-Munk's publishing office in Paris, and he and Jim arrived at a Geneva radio station expecting to be interviewed by a prominent lady interviewer who was something of a European personality.

> She was big on women's liberation, politically very extreme, and she told us she wasn't about to receive us. Here I was with my great friend and author, and she let us know it was a question of his being too crass, too "male chauvinist," too "right wing" in their terms. It was a nasty, gratuitous impoliteness. I was white with fury because there was nothing I could really do. It says something about the integrity of Jim's understanding that he told me afterward, "It don't matter, old buddy."

His non-fiction *Viet Journal*, also published in 1973 by Delacorte, grew out of an assignment from Bob Wool, an editor of the New York *Times Magazine*, to go to Vietnam and write some articles about the wind-up of our involvement there. He went there, the old World War II enlisted man, and the brass treated him royally. A large part of him loved the

United States Army. Some of the older Army—the Army he had known better than anyone of his generation—was still hanging on, but most of it did not really exist any more. That hyped, mass-media war—men going into combat stoned, rock music blaring from radios, all this later to be described by Michael Herr in *Dispatches*—was not his war.

Bob Wool, the editor who sent him to Vietnam, met him in his suite in the Blackstone in New York City shortly after he got back to America. Gloria and Irwin Shaw were also there.

> His suite was full of exotic treasures and souvenirs, nearly all of them for Gloria. He'd brought her back gifts from the Orient—coral and jade, silk and shawls and rings. Like a soldier coming home, I guess, he'd brought back the booty to his girl. About the only thing he brought for himself was in an Army shoulder-bag. Kneeling on the floor, surrounded by the loot, he suddenly remembered it.
>
> "Hey, Irwin!" he said, eyes getting bright. "Just look what I got here." He reached into the khaki bag and pulled out what looked like a large, jagged rock, and set it on the coffee table. Irwin looked down at the thing. "Well, hot shit," he said. "Shrapnel." This didn't put Jim off a bit. He picked it up and tossed it in his hand a few times, as if it were the Hope diamond.

By far the most fascinating section of *Viet Journal*—indeed, one of the finest and most moving pieces of prose he ever wrote—is the long epilogue, in which he describes stopping off in Hawaii to seek the places he remembered from his time there, the time of *From Here to Eternity*. Entitled "Hawaiian

Recall," this unusual essay has an elegaic truth about it, and captures the sadness of three decades gone—of islands, of the sea, of lost youth.

It occurred to him that he could walk into the Royal Hawaiian Hotel, that glamorous institution so inaccessible to him when he was nineteen, and buy anything he wanted. The corner where Maggio had had his fistfight with the two MPs had disappeared entirely. He remembered the times he had watched Air Force pilot officers drunk and fighting on the lawn of the Royal Hawaiian after the Battle of Midway—"or was that Prewitt?" he asked himself. He hired a driver and went around to some of the old streets he had known.

It was amazing. The area had once been a swarming hive of bars, street vendors, tattoo parlors, shooting galleries, photo galleries, market shops, fruit and vegetable shops, and hooker joints occupying the rooms upstairs and labeled hotels. Now there was hardly a soul on the streets, and most of the shops and bars were shuttered and closed. Once it had been our Mecca, toward which we rose and prayed every morning, before Reveille. Compressed into a half-mile area down by the docks between the King's Palace and the little river, and bursting at the seams to break out, it had been the bottomless receptacle of our dreams and frustrations, and of our money. The pay-day payroll. Now it was all coming down soon, the driver said, and an urban reclamation would be built in its place.

Later he looked at the corner bar, now closed, where Warden had come looking for Prewitt when Prewitt went AWOL. The old Chinese restaurant called Wu Fat's was still there, but it was drab and unpainted, and the driver said it was coming down too. It was in Wu Fat's that Maggio had started his final rampage that ended in his going to the stockade. Next door was the New Senator Hotel (he called it the New Congress) where the hooker Alma worked.

He went out to Schofield, to the quadrangle which had been his home for two years. When he came off the stairs and the second floor of the Hq Building, the past appeared again for a moment: "The walls and doors were still painted the same horrible cream-green, and the polished old concrete floor still gleamed . . . The regimental trophy room was in the same place. The administrative offices were the same. And the commanding colonel's office down at the end was the same, his desk in the identical same place, the U.S. and regimental flags behind his desk in their same stands."

The young colonel who showed him around Schofield that day had been a boy in grade school in 1940 when he had served there, and his father an artillery officer. The colonel told him the old caste system was gone. "You couldn't *make* these youngsters do anything, you had to explain to them what you wanted them to do."

On our way back to the Hq Building the young colonel hollered at two troopers who were out washing their car in the barracks street. "I've got one down here that could stand a little polish, when you're through there," he called. The two soldiers grinned. "Yeah? Why don't you grab a sponge and come help with this one?" was the answer that came back. The colonel grinned and winked at me.

Later, I went with a young sergeant who wrote for the Schofield paper, to meet some of the unhappy types, the malcontents, whom he knew and had

worked with. There were five of them sitting around
a four-man cubicle, playing cards on a blanket on the
floor around a candle. The lights had been turned
off. All but one of them wore mustaches, and all of
them had hair longer than was usual. Their com-
plaints, when the sergeant got them down to bare
rock, were primarily that they wanted to wear their
hair and their mustaches even longer. Why, I asked.
"So we won't look so much like soldiers," one of the
boys said glumly. "The girls here don't like soldiers."
Mainly, it came out, they did not like the Army because they were so lonely. In thirty years the song
had changed almost not at all. The past seemed to
rise up and roar at me like a wind tunnel.

The next day, as the plane left the Honolulu airport to carry
him away, he sat alone with his thoughts. "I had come back
hoping to meet a certain twenty-year-old boy walking along
Kalakaua Avenue in a 'gook' shirt," he wrote, "but I had not
seen him."

9.

By 1973 they had been in Paris fifteen years.

It was time now to come home.

The trip back to the scenes in Hawaii may have had something to do with this decision: the feeling of old time passing. Somehow, ineffably, coming home was also intricately associated with his novel *Whistle*, the last of the trilogy—with all the sights and sounds and memories of a vanished America. He was fifty-one, and had been away a long time; perhaps, too, he was just simply worn out with France. And his Paris doctors told him to go somewhere to a warm climate.

Ross Claiborne remembers: "Once, in Paris, I said of *The Merry Month of May:* 'Jim, this isn't one of your major works.' He got very mad at me. But I think in the middle of the night sometimes he must have awakened to the reflection that in

The Merry Month of May and *A Touch of Danger* he wasn't
working at his best, or finding subjects that were challenging
him. I believe he felt he needed to come back to his origins."

Paris itself was changing. The number of Americans there
was decreasing rapidly, a principal reason being the drastic
decline of the dollar against the franc. The French economic
and political crisis also made life considerably less pleasant
than it had once been. Industrial pollution was beginning to
taint the skies. Even Les Halles had disappeared, and
McDonald's had come to the Left Bank.

In *The Merry Month of May* he had written of his neigh-
borhood, the Île St. Louis:

> The Island has become terribly chic, a dozen new
> restaurants have opened up, and the honest poor
> people's tenements have been bought up by entre-
> preneurs and cleaned up and turned into studio
> apartments, where young white-collar executive cou-
> ples, working so hard to build the new Technological
> Consumers' Society of France, now live with their
> narrow black briefcases like a New Yorker's.

Tony Allen, in his *Americans in Paris,* provided the perspec-
tive of the Lost Generation. With the exception of the permanent exiles like Gertrude Stein and Ezra Pound, all of them
finally decided to go back to America.

> For a few, like Thomas Wolfe, who on all of his
> visits to France was dejectedly homesick, the desire
> to get back was immediate and urgent. For most of
> them it was slow-maturing, and it took the incentive
> provided by the Depression to send them home. It

wasn't so much a disillusionment with Europe
. . . It was more a realization that in the long run it
wasn't the place where they belonged.

Fittingly, one of the more flamboyant of the nineteenth-century expatriates, the songwriter John Howard Payne, had composed "Home, Sweet Home" in a shabby apartment in the Palais Royal. The home he wrote about was an old salt-box house four miles down the road from where the Joneses were to resettle in America.

Irwin Shaw would also leave Paris in these years. The more than two decades he lived there, he remembered, had slipped by with more pleasure than pain.

> If I had been a Parisian, responsible for my government and aghast at many of the things that went on in the city, I imagine the ratio of pain to pleasure might have been reversed. But I was never a Parisian. I was always an American, on an extended visit to be sure, who roamed the streets of the city fondly, dined in some of the great houses and in some that were not so great, listened to the gossip and mingled happily with the natives, working with theater people, editors, movie crews, most often in harmony and admiration. Somehow, all during the period when almost every wall was decorated with the sign, "Americans Go Home," it never occurred to me that they meant me.

It must have been painful to give up the splendid house on the Île with all its associations over the years. But one night in 1974 Jim went out with Harry Antrim of a new university, Miami International, who talked with him about coming to

Florida, the scene of so many of his haunts as a young man, to be the writer-in-residence for several months. Jim came back to the house that night and said to Gloria: "I'm homesick. Let's go home."

Rose Styron would remember all those times in Europe:

> I have an echo of Jim and Bill playing the harmonica wherever we were—Biarritz, Florence, Deauville —in the sunshine, on a beach, walking around. I remember when the two of them were playing, I could feel a premonition of death, and that terrible nostalgia that seizes you because it was all so wonderful and sad. It was the premonition one has when there is music and friendship and loyalty, unconnected almost to any place or time—a memory of time itself, of people one loves passing through life.

10.

In the summers of their later years in Europe they had come home for a few weeks, usually to eastern Long Island. One summer they stayed with the Adolph Greens in East Hampton, and another they rented a ranch-style extravaganza in the woods out around Three Mile Harbor with Monique Gonthier and Christopher Shaw. There was a big swimming pool, where Jim taught other people's children, including my own, how to dive. They threw a huge party for their daughter Kaylie's birthday, where they hired a group of Shinnecock Indians to perform. The Indians did, getting very drunk in the process, and finishing their act with the most mindless dirty jokes ever heard at a children's party, such as: "Chief Bowels won't move. Teepee full of shit." One drunk Indian fell into the pool and Gloria had to jump in wearing a new pink dress to pull him out. That summer, 1970, Jim was not feeling well, and Bill Styron took him to some doctors he knew in Boston— the first bulletin of his serious illness.

When they finally left Paris and put up the house on the Île
for sale, they moved to Miami for ten months. Jim took the
job as writer-in-residence at Miami International University.
It was a good way to measure America again; once more he
put his novel *Whistle* aside and was working on the text of the
non-fiction book, *World War II*. Art Weilhas, once the head
art director of *Yank*, had first come up with the idea for this
book. He believed there was much good art about World War
II, and that it was a shame for it to sit in the archives in
Washington where only a handful of researchers could see it.
In Paris earlier, Eugene Braun-Munk had introduced Jim to
Bob Merkel, editor in chief of Grosset & Dunlap, a New York
firm which had had a series of successes with illustrated books
with distinguished texts. "I knew he was having trouble with
Whistle," Eugene Braun-Munk recalled, "and I advised him
that it might be good to get his mind off it and do something
worthwhile that wouldn't take more than a few months."

Sometimes we would all meet in New York City in these
months, at the Blackstone on East Fifty-eighth, and one of our
hangouts was the Dogwood Bar in the hotel. One night Frank
Sinatra, their friend from earlier days, met them there for a
drink, and they left and were walking down the sidewalk toward a restaurant when they suddenly saw two men break the
front window of a jewelry store and make off with some
jewels. The cops arrived almost immediately and began inter-
rogating them as witnesses, and were so flustered to meet
Sinatra that they let the culprits get away. Sometimes they
came out to Bridgehampton. In Miami they rented a house on
Key Biscayne, just three blocks from Nixon's compound, in an
enclave of staunch and rich Presbyterian neighbors. The bank
they used was Bebe Rebozo's. They had a neighbor, a strange
lady, who played Nazi songs on her record player, loud

while the others listen and make comments. I'll read the story aloud to the class and then ask for comments. Then I'll give them my comments on it, and then bring the writer into it, because often people convey something they had no intention of conveying in a piece of writing, without ever having realized it or been aware of it. It's sometimes a rude awakening for a student to realize he's given a totally different impression from what he meant to when he started writing the thing.

On one of my visits to Miami to see them he turned the class over to me without telling me he was going to. Luckily the book under discussion was *The Great Gatsby*, which I had recently reread. Jim sat in a corner smoking his big cigars while I talked for a while and then answered questions. It was obvious the students adored him. But at the end of that afternoon he was exceedingly angry. He stood up to conclude the class. "You been spending all this time asking Willie about how to get literary agents and how to publish stories and how to get publishers. Listen, I been reading your stuff, and as of right now there's only about three of you who know anything about how to write, and you three got a pretty long way to go. You got to read good things and work before you start thinking about literary agents and all that crap."

One of his favorite students was David Gelsanliter, later to be with the Philadelphia *Inquirer*. "Show me the sympathetic insurance man," Gelsanliter remembered he used to say. "Everyone suffers."

In his writing class, Jim seemed to be as concerned with discovering and connecting new things inside himself as with teaching. You sensed that he knew he didn't have much time, so whatever he said, particularly to those he cared about, he tried to get exactly right. "You write with authority and good texture, but you have emotional constipation," he would tell one student. "The problem is that you're not writing about things you know from the inside," he would tell another. Sometimes he would complain in frustration, "I'm not saying it well." His highest accolade would be, "I think that's an absolutely true statement."

"Fiction too often is a tool for the teaching of morality," he would tell us. "I'm still overcoming having been so tough on people when I was thirty. I was right, but I was too harsh and it left scars . . . Write a novel more like life is. Life has no plot."

After class, he liked to visit places where working people went. He would drink white wine and eat saltless steak or fish, overtip the waiters and waitresses, be very gentle with them. He'd tell about growing up middle-class in the Midwest, of taking his parents' values. Then, of going into the Army as an enlisted man and being thrown into the jungle of the common man. Trusting people and getting taken. Squaring off before getting ready to box and being flattened. "Gradually, I came to love the raw vitality of it," he would say to us. "Those on the lower economic level have a much truer sense of life. They're not simply concerned with getting on and all that."

Stewart Richardson, the editor in chief of Doubleday, had heard back in New York that Jim was unhappy that the paperback editions of his war novels had been broken up, that *The Thin Red Line* had not been bought by Dell but was going to another firm, and that he was again considering changing publishers. "Sandy" Richardson, an Easterner who had gone to Washington and Lee, a brilliant, generous advocate of writing, and an admirer of Jones's books, flew to Miami and went to the house on Key Biscayne. He and Jim had never met, but they got along well immediately and did quite a lot of talking:

> He told me, knowing that I was interested in publishing him, that he thought he should tell me in all honesty he would probably have to have open-heart surgery, so he might not be such a good bet as he might appear. I ignored this as a remark that I thought was really cautionary, but not serious. I had no idea of the previous history, going back to 1970. We drank wine, and he showed me his knife collection. When he looked at the knives, he looked at them not as though they were instruments of death or violence, but simply as things that represented craftsmanship and beauty in their own right. They could have just as well been stamps, yet with a great deal more handiwork in them.
>
> After dinner one night Jim gave me about 350 pages of *Whistle*. I took them back to the hotel and read until four in the morning. I was overwhelmed. I told him so the next day. That evening we went to dinner at the house of one of his students several miles away. I found him tremendously patient and gentle, with people of relatively little talent. He was thoughtful and kind to them all. I was reminded of a line from the old comedian Joe Laurie, Jr.: "The bigger they are, the nicer they are."

I respected him enormously for his candor, directness, and a quality of kindness and thoughtfulness that is rare in the literary world. He spoke to me without rancor on all sorts of subjects and all sorts of people. Somehow, by the time I said goodbye, I realized that the one obligation he had was to finish *Whistle*. The day I left Key Biscayne he was standing in the doorway as I got in the taxi. Just before I left he handed me a copy of *Some Came Running* which he had inscribed. The inscription read: "To Sandy, no matter what, Jim."

Jim was intrigued by the Cuban sections of Miami, and loved to drive around Florida to see the scenes of earlier days, and take boats through the Everglades; and it bemused him that his daughter Kaylie had a boyfriend named Stonewall Jackson, who had a mother named Banjo. But I think he and Gloria were a little lonely down there in the end. The doctors in Paris had told him to go to a climate like Florida for his heart. In Miami, the doctors found that a warm climate did not matter. They had already decided to look for an old house somewhere in the potato fields of eastern Long Island.

II.

The eastern end of Long Island, when one lives here year round, bears little resemblance to the Hamptons of the summer society columns of our day. The summer influx distorts its true character. In the off-season it is still a rural place with a quiet village life—anything but a "writers' colony," thank God for that. When the summer ends friends fall back upon themselves and people seem relevant again. It is the beauty of the land which helps hold us together. There are hauntingly beautiful days in the autumn when you feel you do not want to be anywhere else on the Lord's good earth. Little wonder some of America's finest painters chose to settle here years ago. You do not have to go to the ocean every day to remember it is there; the roar of it is never far away. Wherever you first came from, when you leave for a while and then return, and finally cross the Shinnecock Canal, you feel you are coming home.

I discovered the area by accident, from the back of a char-

tered bus years before, with people from *Harper*'s going to
Montauk for a meeting. In a lethargy that day, I glanced out
my window; things flickering obliquely before my eyes
brought me awake: lush potato fields on the flat land, village
greens, old graveyards drowsing in the sun, shingled houses,
ancient elms along the streets, and far in the distance the blue
Atlantic breakers. It was the unfolding of one's profoundest
dreams, and I knew then I would come back someday for a
long time.

It is likely the most lovely terrain in America, and because of that, and its proximity to Manhattan one hundred
miles down the road, I feared it would become a parking lot.
In summertime the New Jersey plates grew more and more
abundant, and this is always a fearsome sign. From an air-
plane flying into the city, one saw the higher civilization coming out this way: earth ripped raw, shopping centers, develop-
ments, all that immense apparatus at the edge of the great
American schizophrenia.

Once at Bobby Van's saloon in Bridgehampton, where Jim
Jones and I and our friends came often, I asked a young potato farmer why he had sold the acreage up the way to W. T.
Grant's, which would install its largest store in the East. "Because my grandmama and I are out for one thing," he said,
"and that's the buck." I could not quarrel with that. Instead,
after a tender silence, on a napkin I wrote from Faulkner's
"The Bear": "The ruined woods we used to know don't cry for
retribution. The men who have destroyed it will accomplish
its revenge." The young landowner, a good fellow, pondered
this message; I could tell he was turning it about in his mind.
Then he said: "I *knew* you were with me."

It is a land that enlists loneliness, and also love. It reminds

me a little of the Mississippi delta, without the delta blood
and guilt—no violence to this land, and it demands little. The
village itself, among the oldest in America, remains part of the
land which encompasses it. It is a place of bleak winters, of
long nights and silences. When my son, as a young boy, came
out from the city he walked all over town talking with the
farmers and the merchants. One day I noticed from my car
this simple tableau: my son on the lawn next to Bobby Van's,
having sandwiches for lunch with Spindley, Bobby's ubiquitous golden retriever. The boy and the dog sat there on the
grass, motionless almost, in the sunshine of a crisp December
noon; the sight of them as I spied on them in their unaffected
pose evoked in a rush my own small-town childhood, and
overcame me with a sadness for mortality.

It is a very small town in the winter, numbering just over a
thousand people. The names of the oldest families reflect the
Anglo-Saxon blood source. Just as the potato fields bring back
the Mississippi delta, the village reminds me of Yazoo, because along the streets, in daylight and in darkness, there are
the sounds of Negro voices, all the vanished echoes of one's
youth. It is nearly 30 percent black, mostly Southerners
brought up a generation or more ago by the farmers, and one
of the sadnesses of the town is that it does not have the despair and cruelty and tragedy of remembrance—the shared
past, the common inheritance of the land. There is an old
Negro man whom we all know, who perambulates around
town at all hours, drinking Thunderbird behind hedges and
trees, talking incessantly to himself, head aslant in his aimless
journey. No one knows where he sleeps, if he does at all.
Eight or ten times a day I see him, one moment down by the
tracks, five minutes later in the graveyard, then near the

church, and I have even sighted him as far away as Sag Pond. Being a Southern boy, I must believe he is a reminder to the town of something it does not truly understand of itself, but then that is a fragile thing. When Jim Jones first saw the old man on one of his endless walks, he said, "I think I knew him in Robinson, Illinois."

There is a fine countermelody of sophisticates and good local people. Once in a restaurant around Christmastime I saw Woody Allen and Diane Keaton dining alone, surrounded by dozens of Rotarians and their wives singing "God Bless America." It is an area abundant in characters—characters of the American species. In the graveyard there is one of them. He and his wife lie juxtaposed under identical new tombstones. The wife's has her name, the dates of her birth and death, and then *Rest in Peace*. The husband's has his name, under that a long serial number, and then *No Comment*. The radio station encourages telephone calls on all matters from local characters, everything from the state of the tides to the rude manners of the New Yorkers, and puts these calls live on the air. Merchants are invited to telephone in their commercials. Once a nursery owner was phoning in his commercial. In the middle of it the announcer interrupted to report he had just received word that a Coast Guard rescue helicopter was on its way to get a sick sailor off a Russian trawler eighty miles south of Long Island. "Go ahead with the commercial, Bill," the announcer said.

> We got hyacinth bulbs, that good Ortho fertilizer, we got spaghetti squash seeds—no, somebody came in and bought the squash seeds. Say, how come the Russians are only eighty miles away? They're not supposed to come within two hundred. What's going

on? Maybe we'd better get some machine guns out there. I don't like squash myself, but we'll have more seeds next week.

I was driving down the road with Jim and Kaylie late one September afternoon three years before, right after the Joneses had bought their farmhouse. The sunlight caught the seared brown of the fields. A flock of Canada geese flew overhead. "God, how I love it here!" he said. With all his appetite for his native land and his native language, he embraced this community and made it his own. His taste for "simple" people, for country ways and country accents, found flourish again. When he first came up from Miami, looking for a house, I introduced him to "Squeak" Lambrecht, owner of the Vogue Beauty Salon. He asked if she would give him a haircut. It was late afternoon, and she opened the shop for him. They talked while Squeak cut his hair. "I'm sick of traveling around," he said to her that day. "I'm through with that fancy French life. I'm coming home."

In the old farmhouse there forever seemed to be laughter, voices of children, wisps of music, dogs barking, something good in the kitchen—and always the presence of literature. Perched there on its hill, it was, he said, "like a ship riding the waves," and it was rumored to be haunted by the ghost of a Mrs. Halsey, who hummed old folk ballads on still nights. Inside there was a poker room, bedecked with Paul Jenkins and Delaney paintings and equipped with chess pieces, Monopoly, Risk, backgammon, and a sinister game of wits called Southwest Conference Football. In a downstairs bathroom was the framed drawing he had done for Burt Brittain's book of writers' self-portraits, and underneath the likeness was his inscription: "Old soldiers never die. They write novels." Next to

167

it was Bill Styron's self-portrait, clad in the uniform of a Confederate major general, and the inscription: "My dear daddy: This is a self-portrait of your son on the day we thrown back the Yankee bastards . . . Cold Harbor, June 3, 1864." Jim and Gloria had knocked out the wall of the front room and made it twice as large, with an enormous fireplace at the end. The French period furniture, the ancient sculptures, and the pulpit-bar with its prayer stools famous to Paris were incongruous in this very American setting, but they worked. One was struck by his sensitivity to finely crafted things, whether objects of furniture or materials of quality—a regard for craft on its own terms: leather items, belts and belt buckles, old American Indian jewelry and rugs, well-carved wood, chess sets, and huge leather chessboards.

One afternoon soon after they had settled in I went up to the big attic where he worked to get a book I needed. It was the summer and Jim was sweating profusely behind his electric typewriter. While he made some coffee I browsed around and saw the following: a long wooden worktable; a bed set in a kind of alcove; several framed poker hands, including one straight flush, the six through the ten of clubs, with the handwritten notation: "Nite Oct. 3, 1967 . . . Stud Poker, Five Card, Called by G. Jones on 5th Card for 50 Fr. bet, Hand Held by Francois Mensurer, Witness Monique Gonthier"; the National Book Award plaque for 1951; a collection of cigarette lighters on a table next to the wall; a framed permanent pass to the Odéon-Commission Cinéma; a collection of walking canes; a bust of Tojo with a pair of sunglasses hanging from his ear; sculptures by Man Ray and Alexander Calder; camera equipment of all descriptions; a framed commission in the Nebraska State Navy; old dart boards; a leather wine pouch from Pamplona; photographs of Gloria and their kids;

trunks full of papers; the framed certificate for the Purple
Heart; dozens upon dozens of bayonets and knives of all sizes
and shapes on a low shelf, including many Randall knives
from Orlando; a framed cover of *Newsweek* for October 1967,
with Bill Styron on the cover; a twelve-inch-square canvas by
Cecile Gray of a mother-of-pearl barrel; boxes of Padrón cigars; a framed membership card for the whole family in the
Club de la Piscine of Deauville; old chessboards, one of them
with a chess problem laid out on it; a framed photograph
from the Robinson newspaper of his family house with a story
saying it was about to be torn down for a parking lot; a collection of belt buckles; a framed bar spoon stirrer with the notation: "From the main bar, Deauville Casino—a veteran of 40
Years' Service—Donated by Owner of Casino—6 Sept. 1969";
and a framed handwritten letter from Romain Gary, which I
paused to read:

April 22nd, 1962

My dear Jimmy,

Just to prove that I mean it, to whom it may concern:

The Thin Red Line, the line between man and
beast, so easily crossed, is a realistic fable, symbolic
without symbols, mythological and yet completely
factual, a sort of Moby Dick without the white
whale, deeply philosophical without any philosophizing whatsoever. Touched by a weird, resigned
and yet light-hearted, ironic, and even optimistic acceptance of our animal nature, with constant flashes
of a sly, dark, peculiar humor, written with a deceptive facility that is the mark of truly great writing,

this extraordinary novel achieves epic proportions through the magic of a joyful love of life and humanity, absolutely unique in contemporary literature. This book belongs to that vein of poetical realism which is the rarest and to me the most precious thing in the whole history of the novel: it is essentially an epic love poem about the human predicament and like all great books it leaves one with a feeling of wonder and hope.

Romain Gary

This entire attic was surrounded by large windows looking down on the open potato fields below. He proudly showed me his view.

Outside the house, a Southern-style gallery with a porch swing overlooked the lawn and the fields beyond. Immense elms, cedars, and flowering bushes dotted the landscape. Off to the side was a set of shrubs and fir trees with an open place in the middle. One day Jim and Jamie and I were exploring these shrubs. "Were you a loner when you were growing up down in Yazoo?" he asked. He was smoking a cigar, and he spat on the ground, apropos of nothing in particular. "I was. I used to hide in shrubs like this and watch the girls go by and think dirty." Just down the road from the house, beyond other farmhouses, were a red one-room schoolhouse and a post office-general store right out of turn-of-the-century America.

Dominating this good old house was a large country kitchen with cupboards and cabinets and kitchen equipment on the walls, and in it the dinner table—a long medieval French piece around which there were many meals lasting into the night, and much conversation. Surely it was not unlike the kitchen Dave Hirsch—the returning soldier, survivor of the

Battle of the Bulge—saw in *Some Came Running*, in Gwen
and Bob French's house in Israel, Illinois:

> It was like a haven, like a haven on a snowy blow-
> ing freezing night. Like in one of those old-fashioned
> Christmas card pictures you always loved to look at
> but didn't much believe in places like that any-
> more . . .
> He could not escape a sudden feeling that here
> suddenly for the first time in his life of thirty-seven
> years he had walked into a place that was safe. And
> the more he looked at it, the stronger the feeling be-
> came. Just safe. That was the only word. Safe from
> what? He tried to analyze from what, but he could
> come up with only the vaguest of generalities. Safe
> from the savageries of frightened men. Safe from the
> witch burnings and destructions of people deter-
> mined by their guilts to prove themselves unguilty.
> Safe from the frightful insanities of reason and honor
> and justice and happiness . . .

I2.

It is saddening that Jim would not live longer to enjoy this place he and Gloria made for themselves. He had had his first attack of heart failure in 1970. The doctors had put him on a salt-free diet and had warned him never again to drink hard liquor. After all the French cuisine, and the scotch and bourbon and martinis, this had to be extraordinarily painful. He switched to white wine, which he could put away in some quantity, and he never gave up his cigars, which were mailed to him from Miami by a Cuban refugee named Pelato in monthly shipments.

"Congestive heart failure is not one of those bland diseases whose course can be measured easily," he himself would write in *Whistle*. It is a gradual failure of the heart, and death usually occurs from it in the fifties, although people have been known to go on living with it for a long time. As it worsens, the lungs fill and one slowly drowns in one's own fluids. He had read much of the literature on it and knew how deceptive it was; the main character in the book on which he was working, Top Sergeant Winch, suffered from the same condition; if Prewitt had been his young man's ideal in *From Here to Eternity*, then Winch was his own shadow stalking him in his decline. Jim was approaching his middle fifties and had no illusions. Congestive heart failure ran in his family. His case was compounded by the serious malaria he had contracted on Guadalcanal, and although he was a young man then, no one quite knew how debilitating this and his war injuries may have been to the system.

Once, several years before, he got into my car with me to drive into Bridgehampton to pick up some Chinese food. "What kind of driver are you anyhow?" he asked.

"Pretty good," I said. "Why?"

"Because I don't want to get killed before I finish *Whistle*."

I mentioned that he had no illusions. But he desperately wished to complete the book he considered the major work of his life. He had first begun actual work on it in 1968, but it went back a much longer time than that. In some notes on an essay, he had once written:

It was conceived as far back as 1947, when I was still first writing to Maxwell Perkins about my characters Warden and Prewitt, and the book I wanted to write about World War II. When I was beginning *From Here to Eternity*, then still untitled, I meant for that book to carry its people from the peacetime Army on through Guadalcanal and New Georgia, to the return of the wounded to the United States. A time span corresponding to my own experience. But long before I reached the middle of it I realized such

173

an ambitious scope of such dimension wasn't practicable.

The idea of the trilogy occurred to me then. *Whistle,* still untitled and—as a novel—unconceived, was a part of it. So when I began *The Thin Red Line* (some eleven years later) the plan for a trilogy was already there. And *Whistle,* as a concept, would be the third part of it.*

Which of course it should be. It was always my intention with this trilogy that each novel should stand by itself as a work alone. In a way that, for example, John Dos Passos' three novels in his fine *USA* trilogy do not. *The 42nd Parallel, 1919,* and *The Big Money* will not stand alone as novels. *USA* is one large novel, not a trilogy.

I intended to write the third volume immediately after I finished *The Thin Red Line.* Other things, other novels got in the way. Each time I put it aside it seemed to further refine itself. So that each time I took it up again I had to begin all over. My own personal experiments with style and viewpoint affected the actual writing itself . . .

There is not much else to add. Except to say that when *Whistle* is completed, it will surely be the end of something. At least for me. It will mark the end of a long job of work for me. Conceived in 1946 and begun in the summer of 1947, it will have taken me nearly thirty years to complete. It will say just about everything I have ever had to say, or will ever have to say, on the human condition of war and what it means to us, as against what we claim it means to us.

---

* Actually, his short novel *The Pistol* could be included in this corpus of work to make a quartet, with his two non-fiction books *Viet Journal* and *World War II* as addenda.

Why did he wait so long to finish *Whistle,* this book which "had kept turning over in its spit in my head for thirty years?" I had the distinct feeling that he knew it would be the last work he could finish. I believe he felt, out of superstition, or some strange intuitive writer's sense, that as long as he was working on *Whistle* he would live—that this book was literally prolonging his life. Yet he was obsessed and, I think, devastated by the finality of what he was doing; in destroying what remained of the old company he was destroying something in himself. In his final months, I sometimes thought to myself that he might die as he wrote the last lines, like Proust. In those last months, the fate of the members of the old company would become so enmeshed with his, with the doom of death, as to be almost indistinguishable, and this in itself was to add an almost unbearable poignancy and drama both to his book and to his life.

In *Whistle,* four wounded members of the old company—Winch, Prell, Landers, and Strange—are sent back from the South Pacific on a hospital ship—"the slow white ship with the huge red crosses on its sides." They are among the first large waves of wounded shipped home. It is early 1943. The serious casualties are segregated in what once was the main lounge—"the repository, the collection-place and bank, of all human evil." The ship docks in San Francisco, just as his own hospital ship had done, and then the men are put on a train to a large military hospital in a fictional city in Tennessee called Luxor, with a close resemblance to Memphis. The novel develops their sense of apartness from other men after the scourge of combat, their fear of recovery and return to battle, their almost animal guilt that they have survived at all while so many among them have not. They are obsessed with thoughts of the mud-smeared platoons still out there in the

Pacific as the war worsens. In their dreams and memories they are haunted by the sound of mortars on fire-scorched hills; the bloody field hospitals; the sight of men of another company and the Japanese killing each other in the pit of a distant valley; the patrols in the jungle at night; the tears of men just back from a firefight streaking the grime on their faces. An embittered loyalty to the old company and the division is their only faith. *Whistle* would be the story of their fate.

Now he was putting in his twelve or fourteen hours a day up in the attic, finishing around sundown, when he would come down for some white wine and a cigar before dinner. I was working on a book too, set in a Mississippi town during another war—Korea—and called, coincidentally, *Taps,* about two teen-aged boys who sound the trumpet for the military funerals, and often at night around the long table in the kitchen we would read to Gloria and to each other—"just trying things out a little," as he would say. His four characters struggling against hope to survive in wartime America made a whole world of their own around the kitchen table on those winter nights. And as his book developed, and I read every chapter as he finished it, I felt the passion in its words.

13.

The book he was working hard to finish was full of blood, suffering, and meanness—the walking dead, the ruined and the maimed—fistfights in bars, all-night parties in the suites of the best hotel, brief and savage sexual encounters, drinking and coupling with the newly liberated town girls just as he and his buddies had done in Memphis in 1943, the altered relationship between men and women resulting from war, the cynical affluence of this country in wartime. Perhaps it is paradoxical that he was trying to finish this life's work in a time when he had at last found the small-town America he wanted so much. There were good moments in this little town, which must have seemed so different from the years in Europe, and what follows here is just a simple litany of some of them.

In the summertime he went to some of the big social parties at first, parties given by rich women, where grown men were known to wear red shoes without socks and lavender leisure suits, but then he pretty much stopped going to them. He never cared much for the inherited rich anyway—as if, for him, they had not really faced the music. "Those damned parties will make a Communist of me," he said. "You have to have a built-in shit-detector to go." He once said to me, of a certain breed of urban intellectuals who attended such parties, "They're city hicks." Everything in his nature rebelled against being an "in group" man. So more often than not he would stay home with Jamie and watch the ball games on television, or you would see him at Bobby Van's at lunchtime, talking with potato farmers or truck drivers or fishermen or carpenters or veterinarians or tree surgeons.

I am a late sleeper, not prone to answer a telephone, and I remember all the countless late mornings he would come round to the back of my house and knock on the window. "Willie Morris! Get your ass out of the sack. Let's go get a hamburger"—or go meet a friend, or take his dog to the vet. One morning, quite early, he got me up to watch Richard Nixon's farewell from the White House the day Nixon resigned. While we were drinking coffee and watching the television in my front room, he went to the door and peered outside. "What are you doing?" I asked. "In damned near any other country there'd be blood running in the streets now," he said. "I don't see none out on Church Lane."

At Chateau Spud there would be spaghetti or Chinese or *choucroute* dinners with Italian wine, hunkering down for hurricanes, poker games every Tuesday night, and TV-watching around the kitchen table. His comments about things on the television screen were sometimes short and vivid. One night a group of literature students from Southampton College were invited to watch the movie of *From Here to Eternity,* which was showing on one of the New York channels. Jim had not seen it in years. In the middle of a scene he suddenly shouted: "Goddam it, I didn't say that!" Another night we were watching a late-night show on ABC about Charles Manson. One of Manson's lawyers, who wore an ill-fitting toupee, was making his case for his client. Manson, he said, was the victim of social forces, and hence innocent. There was a loud, abrupt yell which rattled the kitchen utensils hanging from the walls. "That shithead with the rug is a fake!"

The dinners would be gay, relaxed, full of fun and mischief, and sometimes put together with a few calls on the impulse of the moment. "Informal was not so much the word as unceremonious," he described a dinner at Gwen French's in *Some Came Running*. "There was a sort of catch as catch can quality about it." People might bring dishes, or stop by in the middle of the afternoon to help with the cooking; since Gloria was not noted for her cooking, she had a gift for conning other people into doing it. There was always much talk at the table, and uncorking of wine, with the enormous Swiss mountain dog Wade Hampton and the cats milling around. Their children were usually there, with two or three of their friends from the high school, and other people's children were always welcome—forever an amalgam of the generations, and much amiable banter about the generation gap. If someone arrived late, Gloria would say, "What do you think we are, Spaniards?" Sometimes there would be friends from Paris—Irwin Shaw, Monique Gonthier, Eugene Braun-Munk, Jessie and Clem Wood—and then the conversation would be about those days. But usually these dinners for ten or twelve might include, at one time or another, such good friends who had places in the area as Shirley and Joseph Heller, Keren and Adam Shaw, Bunky Hearst, Jane and Bob Aurthur, Betty

Comden and Steve Kyle, Mike Burke, Addie Herder, Cecile and Buddy Bazelon, Maria Koenig and Peter Matthiessen, Muriel Murphy, Phyllis Newman and Adolph Green, Jack Whitaker, Grace and Warren Brandt, Shana Alexander, John Knowles, Larry Stricklin, Lauren Bacall, or Rose and Bill Styron when they came across the Sound from Connecticut. With the coffee Jim would light up one of his cigars and offer them to others. After that there might be some dancing—Sinatra, Bing Crosby, Glenn Miller, Fred Astaire—often to the records from World War II. Jim had gone down Third Avenue one day to get them at Sam Goody's after he and I had been sitting at the bar of P. J. Clarke's listening to the music from those years on Danny Lavezzo's jukebox.

In the bitter days of winter, there was also an odd inclination toward tricks. I will never reveal the secret, but we devised an elaborate scheme by which someone picks a card from the deck and telephones The Wizard at a local number, and The Wizard tells him the card. We won $9.00 one evening from Adolph Green, who went home cross and dejected. I must confess to being an inveterate telephone prankster, a man of many voices. When the Jones family moved here, they were a great untapped resource for such things: construction crews coming to build a new access road through their back yard, mysterious power failures on the eve of a birthday party, elm trees to be cut down because of the bark blight, friends of friends from Europe arriving to stay for the weekend with six small brats. Once Jim found in his fortune cookie after a Chinese dinner: "You made your wad on human suffering."

One afternoon the honest-to-God genuine cultural attaché to the Soviet Embassy in Washington telephoned Jim. "On behalf of the Union of Soviet Socialist Republics," the attaché said, "we wish to invite you to our country to speak to our college students about American writing."

"Oh, go fuck off, Willie."

There was a long pause. "I beg your pardon?"

"I'm up here in the attic trying to work. Just go fuck off."

The next day the Soviet official telephoned again. "I talked with some strange person on the phone yesterday by mistake," he said. Realizing the man was who he said he was, Jim tried to explain to him that he had a friend who sometimes talked in a Russian accent, but when this was greeted with silence he had to apologize, undoubtedly against his better nature, since he never especially liked Communists.

We have a softball team here in the summers called the Golden Nematodes, named after the microscopic potato bugs which attack the young potato plants without succor or mercy —an amalgam of bartenders, potato farmers, writers, and teen-agers, a team of unusual ethnic diversity held together by Jeffersonian democracy and the double steal. We play on Sunday afternoons in gold-colored shirts and caps behind the Bridgehampton school, to galleries of village dogs, children, and softball groupies, on the same field where Carl Yastrzemski once hit his memorable line drives as a boy. These languid Sunday afternoons might have made a perfect scene for Norman Rockwell were it not for the violence and profanity that were customary. For a while, before he grew more ill, Jim played first base; he was held in high affection by his teammates. On one of these afternoons we were playing a benefit game against a Sag Harbor team for the animal shelter fund. A crowd of about two hundred people turned up, and there was even a public-address system. The game was going in our favor, and in the late innings Jim and I decided to insert a diminutive black kid into center field. We got one of the young white local boys to write down our substitute's name and take it to the public-address announcer. Momentarily the announcer left his post and came up to Jim and me, trailed by the local white boy. "I can't announce *this*," the man said. He showed us the piece of paper, on which was written "Coon Gamble—center field."

"We got a problem," Jim said. "Ain't he got a real name?"

The white boy said, "Yeah, but Coon's the nickname he calls himself."

"Any other names?" Jim asked.

"Well, sometimes we call him 'Jew-Baby.'"

"*Jew-Baby?*"

"His real name's Julian, so Jew-Baby's for short."

"I think you better call him Julian," Jim said to the announcer.

"This is my last game," he said to me one day. "My legs have give out. Besides, my adrenaline gets flowing, and I want to win so bad I can't get back to work the next day." Early on, a batter for the opposing team, safe on a close play at first base, ran him down. Jim held onto the ball, and did not complain, but he got up limping badly. The next batter hit a grounder close to second base. Adam Shaw, the sturdy second baseman, put his foot on the bag and then proceeded to knock the base runner into short right field, this to the admiration of Rick DePetris, Billy DePetris, Yummy DePetris, Joe Luppi, Cal Calabrese, Otis Glazebrook, David Morris, Firpo Rana, Julian Gamble, Bunky Hearst, Jamie Jones, Johnny Angel, Wyndham Robertson, Eddie Pierzynski, and other teammates. "I couldn't let the bastard get away with that," Adam explained. After the Sunday games we would go with our opponents to Rick's Bar on Main Street, all of us, and have frosty mugs of beer and discuss the events of that day's game. The two songs which people always seemed to play on Rick's jukebox on those late days of summer were "The Way We Were" and "The Whiffenpoof Song," the latter with its words: "Gentlemen songsters off on a spree, doomed from here to eternity."

On the cable television at my house on Church Lane one evening there was a showing of *Gone with the Wind*. I invited a few friends over. Gloria and the children were in the city, and he came alone. "I haven't seen the fuckin' thing in twenty years," he said, "but mainly I want to see it at the same time that damned Willie Morris from Mississippi does." He liked my story about my grandmother, who told me she had seen *Gone with the Wind* eighteen times, and the last time she saw it she went just to look at the furniture. He sat on the sofa that night with my dog Pete next to him and took off his shoes and socks, chewing on his cigar and watching closely, spitting every now and again into a brass spittoon. In Atlanta when the camera moved away from the railroad station with its dead and dying and the tattered Confederate flag in the fore-ground and the sound track breaking into a mournful "Dixie," he turned around to us and said, "I think I better go out into the back yard with Pete before I embarrass myself."

One night around Christmastime at Chateau Spud, my son David, Jamie, a friend of theirs named Jay, and Jim were playing Monopoly on the floor by the fireplace in the front room. A large pot, almost $5,000, had built up in Free Park-ing. "We were really killing ourselves to land on it," David remembered. Jamie was on St. Charles Place and rolled a nine, which meant he would have landed on Free Parking. "Jamie got very excited. But Jim's eyes lit up and he shouted,

183

'Hell, no, you rolled an *eight!*' Jay and I picked up on that. We flustered Jamie so much, we convinced him he'd rolled an eight and had landed on New York Avenue. The next day Jamie had second thoughts."

In the summers or early fall we would organize cookouts down at Peter's Pond beach, just a few of us with our children and dogs. We would all get there an hour before sunset, and Jim and I would dig two holes, one for the fire and one for the cooking, and cook a mound of hot dogs and hamburgers. Then we would sit around the fire and listen to the tides and watch the sun disappear into the darkening Atlantic; and, if we were lucky, wait for a full moon to ascend and make what Jim called a "moon's path" on the waters. Someone would have brought a radio, and he was one of the few people I ever knew who loved as much as I to listen to the college football scores on Saturdays in the early fall drifting in from everywhere—first the little Eastern schools like Bowdoin or Colby, or Allegheny and Gettysburg and Susquehanna, on down to the Southern and Midwestern ones which really mattered, then slowly westward—a roll call of America. "There's a poetry of its own in that, ain't it?" he said, while all around the fire the children would be singing songs or telling stories. He never tired of my giving whatever children were on hand the call words of the radio station I worked for as a boy: "This is WAZF, 1230 on your dial, in downtown Yazoo, with studios high atop the Taylor-Roberts Feed and Seed Store." Until he began having attacks of breathlessness, he would help organize one of these cookouts on a moment's notice.

It is an area dominated by the wind. Since eastern Long Island is a sliver of land, divided into two forks and surrounded by two great bodies of water, the wind plays curious tricks, bringing on a quick rainfall without warning, or fogs so thick one has trouble driving. The farmers talk constantly of the wind. The winter grass in the open fields will be creased in the wind just as the ocean will be. One day I watched a monarch butterfly fighting against the wind until it was gradually wafted far out to sea.

There can be much worse than that. One late summer the eye of a major hurricane, one of the most dangerous in years, was predicted to come close to the village. That afternoon the main street was deserted and ghostly still and an eerie orange glow had set in as Jim and I and our sons drove toward his farmhouse with provisions: canned food, water, flashlights, candles, hurricane lamps. He was a good man in an emergency, and stored some of the things down in the cellar just in case. Then we all sat down around the kitchen table, everything battened down and even the cats strapped to something secure, and listened to the screaming wind and the roar of the ocean from afar and watched the trees swaying into contorted silhouettes. Huge branches crashed on the lawn and small objects flew by outside and the big dog began to howl, and then all the lights went out. As we sat there at the mercy of all God's elements in that unholy mutual whine, Jim made a giggle of nearly atavistic joy, as a man who had seen and heard much worse would, and said: "Well, kiss my ass if *this* ain't a show!"

Jim's eternal search, as he once wrote, was for "some nice quiet dimly lit old-infantryman's dream of a bar somewhere." That place for him was a saloon named Bobby Van's, an angular structure on Main Street with dark paneling, Tiffany lamps and old fans suspended from an undistinguished ceiling, a long mahogany bar, and from the back the flickering of candles on small booths and tables covered with red table-cloths—then, too, a covered porch outside named "Nematode Hall" after our softball team, or perhaps named after the potato bugs themselves. It is a village of dogs, big country dogs with friendly faces who roam about unencumbered—all honored local personalities—and it is indicative of the notability of Bobby Van's that they hang around outside, led by my own dog Pete.

I first met Bobby Van one night several years before. He was standing guard over a corpse, a drunk man run over on the road outside, and while we waited in this deathwatch for the coroner, I learned that Bobby was a dropout from the Juilliard School, a pianist since the age of five who decided somewhere along the way that he wanted his own baby grand in his own bar.

He is a native Long Islander, a short dark young man in his thirties, with a look in his eye of the hunter squinting out from the brush: loyal to all, full of good graces, well-brought-up as we would have said in the South. He wears a white chef's suit when he is cooking in the kitchen, and he comes most to life when he is playing his piano—at home with Rachmaninoff or Cole Porter—sometimes in the summers to a packed house of New Yorkers who have frightened the locals away, but in the winters to a handful of us who come in out of the cold.

Bobby knows the tempos and cadences of his native place—a place that, being a resort in summer, changes character more drastically with the seasons than any stretch of earth I have ever known. Only once had I seen him embarrassed by the treacheries of nature here, when the Coast Guard hauled him in after he was lost while fishing in Gardiners Bay for eight hours. (Several of us waited anxiously in the saloon for word of him, meanwhile helping ourselves to free drinks.) He knows the flight of the geese and the next change of the wind. People come there to find out where the bluefish are running or for the baseball scores, they wander in with ducks they have shot to be dressed and eaten, and like our predecessors who sought out deep caves and built fires in them, we came to Bobby's to huddle together during storms. Like the land, there is not much violence in Bobby's either—only occasionally. Once a gentleman threw a coffee cup across the room at me, for reasons not to be disclosed, and with an aim so erratic it clipped Bobby Van on the ear in the middle of *Rhapsody in Blue*. One night very late Bob Dylan wandered in alone and began composing a song on the piano about Catfish Hunter. The local Lions Club meets there; some patrons have been known to go unshaven; and my black Labrador Pete, the official mayor of Bridgehampton, who does his rounds regular as a metronome to check on his constituents, makes Bobby's his last and most significant stop. Pete, once described by a friend as the only black Labrador on Long Island with a Southern accent, opens Bobby's door with his nose, and the men at the bar turn and say, as Jim Jones did: "Here comes the mayor. Good afternoon, your honor."

When Bobby Van married Marina Barone, the place deepened in its dimensions. She was a lovely Italian girl, Long Island product and graduate of Hunter College, and she brought the community even more together: a friend and adviser to our children, an expert on the illnesses of our dogs, a caretaker of the sick and the hurt. She laughed at the occasional cruelties of the town and suffered with them; she brought her tenderness to the life which surrounded Jim Jones's last years.

187

There was a remnant of the Joneses' Paris habits in their long lunch-hour breaks at Bobby's and in the cafe life at night. Jim would order white wine—later grapefruit juice on the rocks—at the bar and a couple of unvarnished hamburgers, and then lean back with a cigar and talk, sometimes with special friends like Joe Heller or Bob Aurthur, sometimes with anybody who wanted a conversation. As Maxwell Perkins once said of another of his writers, Thomas Wolfe, "he loved the loose, expressive language of natural people at a bar when their tongues are loosened a little or much and they speak in the language of life."

Bobby Van, who also served in the 25th Infantry, in Vietnam, became a subject for a certain levity because of his hypochondria. He always had pains somewhere. Sometimes he carried in his pocket X rays of his sinus condition to show his friends, or of his damaged wrist which he broke one celebrative night climbing a tree outside the saloon. Jim would walk up to Bobby and ask, "How are you today, Bobby?" and without giving him time to reply, add: "That's too bad." Then he would turn to somebody and say, "All's right with the world. Bobby looks awful today." Bobby's wife Marina would take her three big dogs to the beach every morning, the dogs poking their heads out of all the windows and causing the tiny car to tilt with their exertions. Jim would arrive at lunchtime and say to her: "I saw you on Ocean Road this morning with them dogs. Them fuckin' dogs are runnin' your life."

On New Year's Day Bobby Van would have open house for the college football bowl games and invite the regular local clientele to bring dishes to supplement the ones he and the kitchen had prepared. We arrived in a good mood that day, since Jim and I were well on our way to winning $400 apiece on four bowl games in a row. We greeted the mingling regulars and then gazed at the long rows of food on the buffet tables. "It sure don't make me miss the Deux Magots much," he said.*

At the bar he would always look the people who came up to talk with him in the eye and talk about whatever they wanted to. Joe Luppi, a graduate of the University of Connecticut and one of Bobby's bartenders, said:

> Anytime I was curious about a certain writer's work, Jim would talk with me about him. He wasn't opinionated, just very concise, but never wishy-washy. He knew his feelings. He was inquisitive about the simplest practical things. We'd talk about food recipes and how to season a daube of beef with dill for a long time. That daube of beef would come up often when we talked. He couldn't use salt, and he appreciated something good-tasting that didn't include it.

---

* Allow this indulgence in listing the dishes that Bobby and the customers laid on for that day: Warren Brandt's samp, Richard Ryan's chili, Willie and David Morris' John Birch Society beans (so named for the intense internal reaction they produce), "Squeak" Lambrecht's meatballs, roast suckling pig garnished with pineapple, herb meatloaf, 25-pound roast turkey with fruit dressing, 35-pound bass stuffed with scallops and shrimp, crab claws, sauerbraten, stuffed clams, venison, pheasant, smoked bluefish and whiting, cured Kentucky ham, Johnny Angel's lasagna, Gloria Jones's turkey hash, shortribs, chicken tetrazzini, chicken cacciatore, roast pork with bean sprouts, salmon loaf with cream cheese and chestnuts, spinach quiche, scallops, cole slaw, macaroni and bean and potato and mixed green salads, oatmeal and blueberry and banana and Irish soda and cranberry and raisin breads, rice pudding and tiered rum cake and cold strawberry and pumpkin soufflés.

Miriam Ungerer, who writes cookbooks and lives down the road in Sag Harbor, would remember:

> Of all the images of James Jones, I suppose the least likely is of this tough old bantam mixing up a salad dressing. Yet that's one of my memories of him: in for his lunchtime hamburger at the bar, thoughtfully stirring vinegar and oil into a dab of mustard. This ritual was probably a little baffling to the summertime gawkers in Bobby Van's, who couldn't possibly know the reason for Jim's custom-made vinaigrette.

Wilfrid Sheed, a neighbor and gifted novelist—*A Middle Class Education, People Will Always Be Kind, Transatlantic Blues*—would see him frequently in Bobby's:

> Silhouetted in the doorway, he looked like a statue of a GI—the eternal dogface who fights the world's wars and eats the world's shit; who dies and is forgotten and turns up right on time for the next one. Jaw way out, feet planted, eyes wary: ready for a fight or a laugh, whichever was on today's agenda. He looked as if he had just stolen the colonel's cigar and was smoking the hell out of it. And when the statue spoke, all the gravel and sand of the parade ground were there, demanding a white wine or asking how the hell you were making out in this lousy world.
>
> The statue was a work of art, and only an artist could have produced it. Up close, Jones was the gentlest of men. His fighting days were over, he'd done all that at the right time of life for it, and he had

some of the lazy assurance of a prizefighter with nothing left to prove. If a brawl *had* broken out, he would either have watched it with interest, or broken it up if it turned ugly.

Still he kept the GI style—as an act of allegiance, and of imagination. At Van's, he hunkered at the bar with whoever fate had sent him. Although he loved writers, with the romantic passion of a Scott Fitzgerald, he hadn't come out here to write about writers. If plumbing or aluminum siding was your game, so be it. He'd talk about that.

Standing with him on his lawn one night, listening to 1940s records, I had no trouble transporting myself to a cramped stage-door canteen, with GIs racing the clock to get drunk and get laid and to forget what they'd seen and what they had still to see. While other people are forgetting, artists begin remembering. And Jones the writer was born back then, the spitting image of his subject (which is a lot better than looking like a writer), but of course much more than that: a funny, grouchy, courteous guy who lived exultantly in the present. Oddly enough, I never heard him talk about World War II. He didn't have to.

One lunch Jim and I and my black dog Pete were at the bar with Jack Whitaker, the CBS sports commentator, who had built a house over by the ocean and named it Sparrow Hall, for the Venerable Bede's sparrow who flew into the lighted hall and out into the darkness again. Whitaker, a gentle and learned man, remembered Jim's face looked like an old Gil Hodges glove—"leathery, mellowed, marvelously lived-in." Whitaker had been browsing through a poetry anthology that morning and was excited to rediscover a poem he had known and memorized years ago in college in Philadelphia; he asked Jim if he knew of a poem entitled "What Thomas O'Boule Said in a Pub" by James Stephens. Unhesitatingly, but with precision, Jim recited word for word all three stanzas:

> I saw God. Do you doubt it?
>> Do you dare to doubt it?
> I saw the Almighty Man. His hand
> Was resting on a mountain, and
> He looked upon the World and all about it:
> I saw Him plainer than you see me now,
>> You mustn't doubt it.
>
> He was not satisfied;
>> His look was all dissatisfied.
> His beard swung on a wind far out of sight
> Behind the world's curve, and there was light
> Most fearful from His forehead, and He sighed,
> "That star went always wrong, and from the start
>> I was dissatisfied."
>
> He lifted up His hand—
>> I say He heaved a dreadful hand
> Over the spinning Earth. Then I said, "Stay,
> You must not strike it, God; I'm in the way;
> And I will never move from where I stand."
> He said, "Dear child, I feared that you were dead,"
>> And stayed His hand.

In an early afternoon of summer Whitaker, who was an infantryman in Europe when he was eighteen, looked across the room and saw Jim and Irwin Shaw standing together at the bar. "That was my war in those two novels those men wrote," Whitaker said. "You could tell they were close friends—no animosity, no bullshit. You could sense the great affection be-

With William Styron, 1974.
(Gloria Jones Collection)

1973, in Paris. From left to right: Bodil Nielsen, Rose Styron,
Irwin Shaw, Gloria Jones, and William Styron.
(Photo by Michel Ginfray—Gamma)

Three old friends: Irwin Shaw, William Styron, and James Jones on the balcony of the Paris house, 1974.
(Photo by Michel Ginfray—Gamma)

Jamie and Kaylie on the balcony in Paris, 1968.
(Gloria Jones Collection) .

Party at the Joneses', 1974. The violinist is Aaron Rosand.
(Gloria Jones Collection)

The view from the Paris house.
(Gloria Jones Collection)

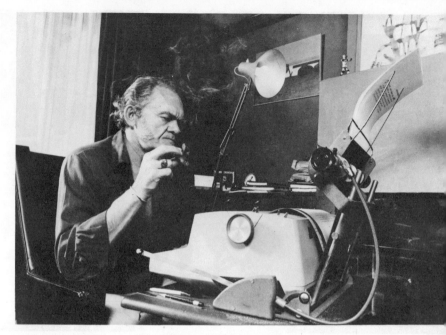

In his study in Paris, 1973.
(Photo by Roger Picard)

With Eugene Braun-Munk and Elizabeth Weicker Fondaris in
East Hampton, 1974.
(Gloria Jones Collection)

James Jones, Truman Capote, Willie Morris, and John Knowles
at Bobby Van's in Bridgehampton, 1975.
(Photograph © by Jill Krementz)

"Chateau Spud."
(Photo by David Morris)

James Jones, 1975.
(Gloria Jones Collection)

OLD SOLDIERS NEVER DIE.
THEY WRITE NOVELS.

BLACKSTONE
Jan 17, 1975.

Self-portrait, 1975.

James Jones, Bridgehampton, 1975.
(*Photo by David Morris*)

tween them. Seeing them like that together made me feel good."

Billy Gillan owned a frame shop next door to the saloon, and had seen a lot of people come and go in that place. "The first time I saw him," Gillan remembered, "he came in and kind of stood there silently. I had no idea who he was. But I knew just by looking at him that this guy had paid his dues. He was like a streamlined cat, a street fighter." Later they would get to talking at lunchtimes. Gillan had been in the U. S. Marines, and for a time served as a guard in the notorious naval prison in Portsmouth, New Hampshire:

> He was interested in that prison. He said, "I knew the brig-rats at Schofield Barracks." I told him half the guys who were guards should've been behind bars. He said he knew exactly what I meant.
>
> He'd really talk when he brought out his cigars. He always offered me one. Good cigars are hard to part with, and this told me something about the man. From the first day I met him I was overwhelmed by what he knew about everything, his honesty and respect for my own individuality. We talked one day about the pain of being human, the way all people have to go through pain. We both agreed you had to know real pain to know real compassion. We also laughed a lot about the way we both hated our mothers. He said there were a lot of days he'd sit down at the typewriter scared to death, but he'd been doing it so damned long he'd learned pretty much to live with the fear. One afternoon he came in with joy all over his face and said, "I been working

on a paragraph all fuckin' morning and I finally got it the way I wanted it." He was fascinated with the details of a scuffle I got in at Bobby's a couple of nights before, when two guys thought they wanted to kick my ass for telling the truth. We went a few rounds and it finally cooled out. He asked me all about it and laughed his tail off. Then he told me he didn't fight any more.

But there was one time, when he was sick. A spoiled, rich man, always dressed nattily and noted for the vast properties he had acquired during the Depression, came up to the bar at lunch one day and fondled Gloria on the breast. Jim, standing there next to her, turned to the man and said, enunciating the words: "If you do that again, you sorry shit, I'll deck you."

One day he and I were having lunch in Bobby's. A fellow came by and said, "Hi, Jimmy!" and he said, "Hi, there."

Then he said to me, "I hate it when people call me Jimmy. Don't never call me that. I wouldn't name an old dog Jimmy."

"How would you like a name like Willie?"

"That's different. That way we don't know if you're white or black. It sounds like a halfback, or a sprinter. Hell, you're lucky."

One of our neighbors and friends was John Knowles, a gracious West Virginian, Yale man, and author of such novels as *A Separate Peace*, that memorable tale of growing up, of pain and betrayal; "Jack" owned a big, smart German shepherd named Clyde, who he said was writing a book called *A Separate Dog*. One summer afternoon the photographer Jill Krementz had arranged to photograph Jack Knowles, Truman

Capote, Jim, and me in front of Bobby Van's. When this session was over, Knowles had to leave to feed his dog, who was lately getting into trouble for making off with golf balls from a golf course abutting his house. Capote was likewise a neighbor, with a place near the ocean in Wainscott; he asked Jim and me to have a drink in one of the front booths.

In the dying sunlight we sat mesmerized as Capote, in his wide-brimmed hat, began telling us, in the most graphic detail, and in his brilliant, affectionate way, all about his bizarre family from Alabama. I had known and liked Capote for a long time and considered him a friend, but had never once heard him open himself so like that, about his parents, aunts, uncles, cousins, and himself there in the Southland: we learned, for instance, that his mother had once been "Miss Alabama," years before she committed suicide, and that one of his cousins was a professional parachute jumper. When he was growing up down there, he said, kids did not bother him even though he was very small because, he said, he had the fastest tongue in the South. It may seem rather incongruous, the little fellow with the lisp in the wide-brimmed hat talking there with the supposedly macho busted-down sergeant with the cigar about Alabamian aunts and uncles—and about his time in the Quarter in New Orleans, and the months he spent in a motel room in Garden City, Kansas—but then it really wasn't; the men who wrote *In Cold Blood* and *The Thin Red Line* knew mutually of life's shadings and extremes. We must have sat there in the booth for a couple of hours, long after the sun had gone down and Bobby Van began to play "Moon River," and then some Cole Porter, listening to Truman Capote spin off this intriguing Balzacian tale, sometimes asking questions when he faltered or took a rest between his pirouettes, which would get him back onto the subject again. "Southerners always go home, sooner or later," he said, "even if in a box." It was that kind of saloon.

There was a day, too, in the crowded summer when a young married couple we knew and cared for had one of those elemental crises which would soon lead to divorce. Jim had been with the young man, the son of a close friend, for a long time that afternoon, talking about life and love. Gloria had been with the young woman; then it had been my turn. Later I met Jim and Gloria on the porch at Bobby Van's. As I approached their table, he extended his arm in a gesture of self-defense. "It's killing me!" he said. "I'm all churned up inside. Let's talk about something else, nothing on the human heart." Then, as I pulled up a chair, he sighed deeply. "We're all so goddamned fragile," he said.

He was enjoying watching his children grow up in America. Both Kaylie and Jamie were enrolled in the high school in East Hampton, six miles away. Kaylie was strikingly beautiful and had become involved in the local theatrical group, and her parents attended every production she was in at the Bridge-hampton Community House. Jim, I believe, was a little in awe of her beauty; awed, too, by his sense that they were so temperamentally alike; he loved her very much. One night at the Community House, when Kaylie and my son David had roles in a musical called *Little Mary Sunshine,* we were all sitting in a back row. Jim got up in the middle of the first act to go down front. "I got to see her a little better," he said as he left. I think he was amused and gratified when Kaylie, at the age of fifteen, decided that she wanted me to be her "godfather" for life, on the grounds, she explained to me, that I loved her too, and that she thought her father and I were such buddies and so much alike.

When his son Jamie was a small boy in Paris, he and Jim had been watching a war movie on television. "Is that the war you made all your money on, Dad?" he asked. Between the two of them there was a rough-and-tumble, irascible kindness. Jamie was a handsome young man, thoughtful and kind, with a wry humor that constantly had us laughing. He also enjoyed mimicking my Southern accent, and then began to like it so much that he more or less talked that way all one summer.

Jim and I talked often of the relationship between fathers and sons—"a delicate and good sort of thing and one of the best," he said, "and also very strange." Jamie was interested in sports, in mastering the rules of football and baseball and track, and on late Saturday mornings in the autumn Jim and I would go sit in the bleachers at the East Hampton school and watch him on the junior varsity football team. One summer afternoon our friend Jack Whitaker took all of us to see a New York Mets baseball game at Shea Stadium, where the television announcer Lindsey Nelson was our host. We had preferential treatment and were ushered in through the press entrance. Inside, people were whispering and pointing to Willie Mays as he signed a few autographs. Jamie, a child of France, motioned me off to the side of the room and asked, "Who's Willie Mays?" My son David was in high school in New York City but was in Bridgehampton often; he was part of this family group. One summer he worked as a cub reporter on the East Hampton *Star* and did a piece on Jim about the work he was doing on *Whistle*. He adored Jim and liked most of all listening to him talk; since David was a humorous young man himself, I believe he considered Jim one of the funniest men alive. Too, Jim had a way with young people, treating them

always as equals, explaining things without a trace of conde-
scension, and not allowing them to get away with much nonsense.

One winter night Jim and Jamie and I were sitting around
the kitchen table talking. We had been discussing something
about the war. Jamie asked: "Why haven't you ever showed
me your medals, Dad?"

"Because I don't believe in that shit," Jim said.

"Where are they?"

"Tucked away in some drawer in the attic, I guess."

"Well, I'd like to see them."

Reluctantly he trudged upstairs and rummaged for a while.
Jamie and I heard the thud of big objects from the floors
above. Then he came back with a box. He sat down at the
table and brought out an assortment of ribbons and medals
and blew the dust off them. Jamie wanted to know what each
one was.

"This here's Good Conduct. They took that one away once
and then give it back . . . This is for Guadalcanal." An
orange-and-red-striped one was the Asiatic-Pacific campaign
ribbon and medal, with a bronze star on it for Midway. Another was the yellow American Defense ribbon, with a battle
star, he said, for Pearl Harbor.

"What's this pretty one?"

"That's the Bronze Star."

"And this one?"

"That there's the Purple Heart. But this one here, it's the
only one we wore when we shipped home." He pointed to the
replica of a rifle on a field of blue with a silver wreath around
it. "It's the Combat Infantryman's Badge."

"Why is it the only one you ever wore?"

"Oh, shit, I don't know. It was a point of pride, you see—

better than all the rest. It spoke for itself. It really meant something. It was just an unspoken rule. If you wore any of the others, the men would've laughed you out of town, or maybe whipped your ass."

There were the many nights with a few of us sitting around the kitchen table talking or reading out loud. The subject at hand might be just about anything. Once, talking about love, he enunciated what he called Jones's Rule Number One. "The one that leaves first wins. The one who's afraid of the other one leaving is the one who's already lost." Or he said: "If women really knew what they have between their legs, they'd run everything. Shit, they do anyway." Or he described the first time he watched the Hollywood version of *Some Came Running*, when in an early scene Frank Sinatra, playing the rather seedy and uncertain war veteran Dave Hirsch, suddenly emerged from a convertible in the small Illinois town wearing an elegant button-up cashmere sweater. When Jim saw Sinatra in that sweater, he said to himself about the movie: "Oh, oh. We're in trouble."

For several mornings one summer Cecile Gray used their back yard in Sagaponack to paint a landscape. "Every morning he would come out and watch me work, always asking pertinent and intelligent questions, observing my point of view as it would differ from what he saw from the same vantage point." That night, discussing music with Cecile's husband Bud Bazelon, Jim said: "You composers live in a world of sound dreams."

One of his favorite set of records was an album on the Civil War, with the songs from both sides. One night, as some of us sat drinking wine and listening to the music, he read from a young soldier's letter to his family, written the night before he went into battle at Fredericksburg. Suddenly the tears started coming. None of the rest of us cried, but we were saddened by his sadness. They were not the tears of a man in his cups; he was dead sober, and dead earnest, and his tears overran the frivolity in the room.

He loved the last two paragraphs of his non-fiction book *World War II*, and would read them aloud every now and again to us when the mood was right. These concluding paragraphs came under the final heading "Pass in Review!"

> How many times they had heard the old, long-drawn-out, faint field command pass down the long length of vast parade grounds, fading, as the guidons moved out front.
>
> So slowly it faded, leaving behind it a whole generation of men who would walk into history looking backwards, with their backs to the sun, peering forever over their shoulders behind them, at their own lengthening shadows trailing across the earth. None of them would ever really get over it.

In a measure, this impressive book *World War II*, with the art and illustrations from the war, marked his return to America. Published in 1975 by Grosset & Dunlap and including many autobiographical passages which were among the best words he had written, it was accepted by a whole generation of Americans who he thought did not know him. He made a promotion tour around the country for the book—television, radio, book-signings—and I believe he saw then how deeply his work had been absorbed into the consciousness of America; he was honored and gratified, and it made him feel good after the many years abroad, that his writing was appreciated so widely.

One night late, Jamie and David and I were sitting around dealing poker hands when he burst in through the kitchen door laughing. He had landed earlier at La Guardia from a trip to Cleveland on the book; the publishers had a limousine and driver waiting to bring him the hundred miles home. He had fallen asleep in the back seat. The driver had missed the turn to Bridgehampton and drove all the way to the very end of Long Island—the Montauk lighthouse—with no land beyond it until Portugal. He told us the driver woke him up and said, "What do we do now, Mr. Jones? The damned road's run out." On a Halloween night five or six of us were having dinner at Bobby Van's; Jim was expected to get there momentarily in another limousine from La Guardia after a trip to Chicago. Gloria and Muriel Murphy had bought some false faces at W. T. Grant's. When we saw him come through the front door, we put on the masks, continued eating, and ignored him as he approached the table. He walked up to Gloria and said, unflinchingly: "I know you."

In the national election of 1976, I recall he liked President Ford and was personally inclined to him because of his decency and his example after Watergate. A basically unideological man, Jim worried about Jimmy Carter's fundamentalist religious background as it might affect the advances made in this country in the liberality of the language as it had come to be used by the best writers—the whole inheritance of the language which *From Here to Eternity* had once extended so. He agonized that a rigorous Southern Protestantism might inspire a retaliation against the freedom of writers to use words as they wished and to deal with sexuality without inhibitions. We argued about this, one of the few serious arguments we ever had. "You're just a Southerner," he said. "You want the South to rise again." At first I felt his concern on these grounds reflected an uncharacteristic naïveté, that after so many years abroad he was merely out of touch with the nuances and realities of American politics.

But the more we talked about all this, the more I recognized that his deeply rooted fear of organized government tampering with artistic freedom was the most profound expression of his commitment to the working values of literature —to his passionate faith in the written word and to his unease that in our changeable, disparate nation, our gains as writers, so hard-fought, might be taken away from us, from whatever source and for whatever reason. In the end he decided to vote for Carter, because he said the man had finally impressed him by his strength of character and intelligence, that and by his very secular belief in the diversity of America. Gloria, never very ideological either, even though she had marched in anti-Vietnam parades in Paris, chose President Ford, but having never used a voting machine after the many years in France, claimed she pulled the wrong lever and voted the straight Communist ticket.

There was a Christmas which lingers in my memory as one of the best—a huge tree in the front room of Chateau Spud, with ornaments going back to Paris days, a fire crackling in the fireplace, a turkey in the oven, and outside, on this cold dark afternoon, a touch of snow on the sloping lawn. Friends came and went, and then dinner—Gloria and Jim and Kaylie and Jamie and David and I. Afterward we sat by the fire and read poems and played music and listened to Robert E. Lee's farewell to the Army of Northern Virginia on the record player. Then Jim got down Shelby Foote's *Civil War* and read the speech Oliver Wendell Holmes made at a soldiers' reunion in 1881:

> You could not stand up day after day, in those in-decisive contests where overwhelming victory was impossible because neither side would run as they ought when beaten, without getting at last something of the same brotherhood for the enemy that the north pole of a magnet has for the south, each working in an opposite sense to the other, but unable to get along without the other.
>
> I think that, as life is action and passion, it is required of a man that he should share the action and passion of his time at peril of being judged not to have lived . . .
>
> For one hour, twice a year at least—at the regimental dinner, where the ghosts sit at tables more numerous than the living, and on this day when we decorate their graves—the dead come back and live with us. I see them now, more than I can number, as once I saw them on this earth.

That prompted us to telephone Shelby Foote down in Memphis and wish him Merry Christmas. Then Jim put on another record, one in which he reads from his own work. He played that section in *From Here to Eternity* where Prewitt sounds taps, his voice cracking a little in places. As everyone listened to the record I sneaked quietly into the poker room and got an old World War I bugle from a shelf there and went outside in the snow. I could hear the record from the front room, and just as the section finished I played taps on the bugle as I once had as a boy for military funerals in the Mississippi delta, but faltering seriously on the high notes.

Day	*is*	*done*
Gone	*the*	*sun*
From	*the*	*lake*
From	*the*	*hill*
From	*the*	*sky*
Rest	*in*	*peace*
Soldier		*brave*
God	*is*	*nigh.*

When I went back inside, Jim said: "You ain't as good as Prewitt."

He was an ironic man, full of surprises. He was, of course, an enlisted man in the war, and his books of men at war take the side of the enlisted men against the officer caste, back in those years when the U. S. Army was far from being "democratized," and the enlisted men, so often outcasts from American society, lived under miserable, humiliating conditions. He always wrote out of his feeling for the misery of these men, and from this he never deviated. Many of the most moving passages in *Whistle* would continue this theme; some of its most revealing sections would be about enlisted men and noncoms trying to outwit and manipulate their officers.

He would write in *Whistle:*

> Respect was the secret. No matter what you really thought. All any West Pointer wanted from you was the right to be fatherly. The higher the rank, the greater the father. All you had to do was keep Sir-ing

them, and not be cocky because you had moved up
. . . Cockiness was something they watched for nar-
rowly.

"Soldiers have a great instinct for being suspicious of
kindness," he wrote in *The Pistol.* "Any time things are made
easy for them, they are wary." And when Mast's superior
came to take the pistol away from him out on Makapuu Head,
Mast shook his fist and shouted: "You got no right! It ain't
fair. You got no right to do that to us." Yet he knew, too, what
the Army had meant to certain kinds of men, as in this passage from *Some Came Running:*

> "Raymond, Jesus Christ," Dewey said, with insult-
> ing patience as if counting blocks to a child. "I think
> if you went back to school for ten years you might,
> you just might, if you were lucky, come out of it
> about as smart as a nine-year-old Mongolian idiot.
> Look: You never had it so good as you did during
> the war. You never were so happy and successful in
> your life and neither was I and Hubie. For the first
> and only time in our life, the three of us, we
> belonged to something, to a society, where we had a
> definite place and an important job. We fit. What we
> did was right, and what people wanted us to do. We
> had regular definite things we could do, for some-
> body, responsibilities, definite—and important—jobs
> to perform. All three of us, and the Company Com-
> mander needed us, too. We filled a place. And you
> loved it, and I and Hubie loved it."

I think he was secretly proud to be in the company of colo-
nels and generals. In Paris, though a civilian, he had had PX
privileges, something that other Americans who had been in

the war and had lived there longer than he never had. One of his best friends in Paris, where he was with NATO, and later in Washington, was four-star general Fred Weyand, whom he spent some time with in Vietnam doing his *Viet Journal* while Weyand was commanding his old outfit, the 25th Infantry (he dedicated the book to Weyand and his wife), and still saw from time to time. When the non-fiction *World War II* came out, the publishers gave a lavish party in the Federal City Club in Washington. A sizable portion of the Washington Establishment turned out, including Henry Kissinger, but also large numbers of military brass, generals and admirals on down, all of whom were anxious to meet the author. All this thoroughly amused him. At a small dinner of friends later at the Georgetown Club, it was General Weyand, Commanding General of the U. S. Army, who offered the main toast: "To Pfc. Jones, who understood us all."

So, too, with the critics. Probably no major American novelist had been so consistently damned since Faulkner in the 1920s and 1930s, and a certain amount of this seemed to center on his life-style in Europe, whatever that meant. The Pearl Harbor-Paris connection was obviously disconcerting to more than a few American men of letters. Envy has always had a large part to play in book reviewing, as it does in almost everything else (so do personal grudges and old scores to settle, as well as the desire to create a stir at another man's expense, much more than is generally admitted), and early literary success in this country has often created its own special backlash. Some claimed he was a one-book man who had failed to grow with his work, others—in the cute, catchy language of some reviewing—that he was either a good writer who wrote bad books or a bad writer who wrote good ones. He caused great

unease. Far too many of the assessments of his most serious
work over a quarter of a century were either prim or queru-
lous or mindlessly savage or inane, or all of these. His critics
failed more consistently than he did. He wrote some bad prose
—what good writer doesn't?—but he also wrote some of the
finest lyrical passages in American literature. He worked hard
to bring to perfection a prose style which, though sometimes
on the surfaces awkward, was so direct, honest, and consistent
in its treatment of human beings and the world that it brought
its own moral strength to his narratives. He wrote a couple of
artistic failures, but in the context of his entire corpus of work
this seems minimal, and indeed almost to be expected. One
might have thought him to be hostile and bitter, but this was
not the case. He must have been deeply hurt at times, like an
old boxer accumulating a lifetime of body blows. The example
often held before us is that of Faulkner, so Olympian that he
never read the reviews of his books, but when once asked why
he disdained them, he replied that he had read them at one
period in his life and they hurt so much that he stopped.

"I think the critics always concentrated on what they considered the stylistic flaws in his writing," his last editor, Ross
Claiborne, recalled, "—the heaviness, the repetitions, missing
often the talent."

He was almost categorized from the first book as a
war writer, a writer about soldiers, and wherever he
strayed from this they dismissed him as a man who
couldn't deal with *civilian* themes. I think his being
an expatriate also worked against him in the New
York literary establishment—this hotshot, hayseed
Midwesterner who goes and gets some literary pre-

tensions and settles in Paris and has a "salon." I sus-
pect the people who weren't invited to his house
were particularly jealous of him.

He almost never spoke of critics at all, and when he did he
did so with an almost courtly detachment. I know he believed
as a tough old practicing writer, as indeed do I, that there is a
splendid minority of critics and reviewers in New York City
and elsewhere who take their calling seriously, rooted both in
the great sweep of literature and in their own times, who seek
to understand and uphold fine writing beyond all the fashions
and the temporary meannesses—people who are zealous of the
imaginative word and are comprehending of all that goes into
it; from William Dean Howells on down in America, these are
the best, and they undergird the finest writing of their day as
they always have. I recall Jim and I once talked, for instance,
about the critic Malcolm Cowley, about Cowley's own days in
Paris in the twenties and the honest assessment of the writing
life in *Exile's Return,* and of his collaboration in a very true
sense with Faulkner in *The Viking Portable Faulkner* in 1945
when that writer's work was out of print.

As in most things, Jim was no ideologue. I never heard him
single out a critic or a book reviewer harshly. On reading a
bad review, his mouth would go a little sideways and he
would say, in a kind of tender growl, "It don't matter." And
add: "It's small gunfire." He simply did not have that kind of
embittered resentment over the way he had been handled
through the years that some writers in America have had. He
would never have indulged himself against them as Thomas
Wolfe did when he told Max Perkins he did not "care one
poor Goddamn of a drunken sailor's curse whether I have dis-
appointed the world of bilge-and-hogwash writers or any of

the other literary rubbish of sniffers, whiffers, and puny, poisonous apes." Or as Hemingway, who called them "angle-worms in a bottle" and "lice that crawl on literature." He believed implicitly that the best of his work would endure. He did not make a big matter of this, rather it was nourished by a quiet faith. I think all he expected of the critics was a little more civility and intelligent good manners, that and some-what less scorn and fear of the hinterland. Of his character Dave Hirsch, the writer in *Some Came Running*, he had writ-ten:

> He felt like a badly battered, much scarred, tough old veteran who had served in so many battles of the human ego, and had the wounds and missing parts to prove it, that one more didn't matter. If this battle was won, there would be another next week; and if this war was won, there was sure to be another in five years.

But there is one small moment which I must describe in a little detail, not for the personal aspects, which are not espe-cially admirable, but as an illumination of my friend.

I had been asked to write an introduction to a collection of photographs of the South which was brought out by a South-ern publisher. A long review appeared in the New York *Times* Sunday book section. I would never have read it except that the Southern boys who had brought out the book, and were rightfully proud of it, were curious to know why a five-thousand-word introductory essay had prompted such a bitter personal attack and condemned a pretty good book. Having not had much experience with New York book reviewers, and possessing a fine sense of Dixie fair play, the Southern boys, I feared, were thinking about taking the next Delta flight up to wreck the offices of the *Times* book review.

Reluctantly I bought the paper and read the review. It was written by one of those minor careerists who flitter about on the surfaces of the city, noted chiefly for his pallid essays on nature. I remembered him vaguely from my days there, standing on the fringes of the crowd at parties, scowling. The piece attacked me for greed, self-importance, and a lack of character, and said my well had run dry. It added that I did not understand the South. Not understand the South, indeed! Anyone who has written and published for a long time can expect atrocious reviews. I had been through the mire of Texas politics and was used to raw, brutal discourse directed at me, and at friends. A serious writer must grow, mature, live, and survive with his work—some good, some bad, some great—the old rhythms. But in my years in the trade, this was the most gratuitously malicious attack by one writer on another that I had ever seen.

At first I laughed it off, and with any sense I should have left it at that. But then a couple of mean Texas friends roared into town and we had a few drinks and got on the subject of Yankee snobs and made a wish that Jubal A. Early had had five thousand more cavalrymen in his raid on Washington in '64—one of those nights—and I got angrier than I had been in years, at the mean-spirited nits who sour our difficult calling. I got on the telephone to Jim.

"I want you to listen to what this review said today."

"Go ahead."

I began reading. As the sentences rolled off, I slowly began to discern a curious sound on the other end of the line, one that is nearly impossible to describe. At first I thought he was crying softly, but as I continued reading, listening to the enigmatic sound all the while, it became somewhat more punctuated, like a muffled cackle.

"What are you doing, Jim? Are you *laughing?*"

"I'm sorry. I can't help it."

"Why are you laughing?"

He paused to get his breath. "Because it sounds just like the
things they wrote about me for years. It could be the same
sentences. Hell, the same guy. Probably is." And he laughed
some more.

"Well, hell," I said. I sat there, mesmerized by his giggle.

"Oh, shit, come on," he said, and now the words were tender. "You should know better. You been drinkin'? You should
know by now the little shits like that don't know nothing
about wells runnin' dry because they never had a well to start
with. Ain't it obvious? He probably ain't gettin' much. He's
thwarted and full of rage. That's the asshole story of the
human race, ain't it? I'm surprised at you."

"I guess you're right," I said, for by now I was a little
ashamed of myself.

"Of course I'm right. Get off the phone and go back to
work. We both got work to do." Then he laughed again, his
crazy shit-eating laugh. "What did you do? Make out with his
wife?"

I mentioned that the man and his work were all of a piece.
Yet I sensed that, as a man, he had fought hard to retain his
kindliness against his own deepest feelings as a writer—
nourished by his experience—of the essential malevolence of
human nature. Who are we? Where do we come from? Who
or what put us here to suffer so, and to know ourselves we will
die? We are all part of the animal order, of "Mammalia," as he

sometimes called it. "It all lies in the black heart of the human race," he wrote, "and there's no answer to that." Gwen French said in *Some Came Running:* "You can't get two human beings together for more than five minutes at a time without something cropping up and some trouble of some kind starting, somebody's vanity or ego getting involved, some stupid petty little antagonism." During the December 7 attack on Pearl Harbor, his protagonist in *The Pistol* had these thoughts:

> Standing under the covered porch [of Schofield Barracks] and watching the scene before him, a sad, bitter melancholy crept over Mast. It was a feeling that even the longest life was short and the end of it was death and extinction and then rotting away, and that about all a man could expect along the way was frustration, and bitterness, and phoniness in everybody, and hatred.

He knew, as a man and in his work, that there are savages among us—truck drivers or academicians or executives or bridge-party wives or professional soldiers or the man at the other end of the bar—and that they are part of the human race, of being human, for we all have elements of cruelty in us. On a different level of experience, there are bad people who enter into one's life, and you love them and give them your affection, and then they turn on you out of impulses of destruction. Better to be wary. Particularly the vicious American types, men and women, whom he knew in his very blood, never eluded his sensibility, he wrote about them in his novels and never spared for detail, and he tried to deal with them understandingly in his personal life. He had not let us down in his implicit warning, from Captain Dynamite Holmes and

Fatso Judson right on through: Try not to let the cruel ones take over. Imperfect though we are, *be vigilant* of the best things in our humanity.

One night, in a crowded restaurant on a summer weekend in East Hampton, he said: "I got this fuckin' ear. Just listen. All around us people are knockin' other people."

War becomes the last extension of our incomplete evolution:

> There had to be something somewhere in all of them, in all of us, that loved it. Some dark, aggressive, masochistic side of us, racial perhaps, that makes us want to spray our blood in the air, throw our blood away, for some damned misbegotten ideal or other. Whether the ideal is morally right or wrong makes no difference so long as the desire to fight for it remains in us. Fanatics willing to die for ideals. It was territory, back when we were animals. Now that we have evolved into higher beings and learned to talk, territoriality has moved up a step higher with us, and become ideals. We like it. Cynical as it sounds, one is about led to believe that only the defeated and the dead really hate war. And of course, as we all know, they do not count.

And again:

> But what about "war"? Certainly, it is still with us. Certainly, we have not solved it. I don't think we will solve it, until we solve ourselves. War is a very ambivalent thing. As we ourselves are ambivalent. Even amongst the most pacific of us there are warlike tendencies . . . War is hysteria. And hysteria is infectious; and addictive. As long as one nation or

group is willing to fight another, for whatever reason,
I guess we'll have war. So, as long as one individual
is willing to kill another individual, for whatever
good reason under the sun, our race will war.

It is at least a possibility that in the far-distant future, when we have solved ourselves, when our race
has solved itself, we will look back on the inevitable
loss of war with sadness. And write wailing minor-
key hymns to it and its heroes, and to the lusty vital
race we once were, with melancholy longing. But
you and I will know that that is only myth.

"Could a man—any human, really live and not cause pain—
live his whole lifetime and cause no one pain?" His answer
had been no. We suffer, we learn, and we grow. Anything
which matters brings suffering and grief and pain. Bob
French quoted from the occult after Dave Hirsch's death in
*Some Came Running: "Shun not the cloak of evil, for if you
do it will be yours to wear. And if you turn with horror from
it, when it is flung upon your shoulder, it will cling the more
closely to you."* And each man must find his salvation alone.
"Jim was never interested in word games or suburban
agonies," Peter Matthiessen wrote. "He felt a profound obligation to deal with the great matters of existence as against people's ideas of them, and he confronted with courage and real
power that despair of death-in-life that threatens to overtake
each one of us."

And through it all he had believed somehow in the hope of
human dignity. Prewitt would not go back to playing the
bugle if he had to box again to do it, because Prewitt knew he
had damaged a fellow human being in the boxing ring. "After
all," Dave Hirsch had said, "Ginnie Moorehead might not be

much, but she was still a human being; and as a human being
was entitled to certain rights, to a basic dignity and respect.
He didn't care whether they took her or not, but a hog in a
slaughterhouse was not the same thing as a human being, either."

It was a bleak view, perhaps, yet relieved by the possibilities of kindness, courage, civility, talent, the spirit of fun,
friendship, and love.

I believe he had carried these hopes into the writing life,
and that he thought writers should be somewhat more ex-
emplary than other human beings. "Writing's not a natural
pursuit," he said. "A natural pursuit is to be standing in a field
with clubs and hitting each other on the head." "Literary people"—the literati—could be as malignant and vengeful as anybody else. Knowing great literature should make people a
little more compassionate, but it often did not work out that
way. "Some of the meanest people in the world," he once said
to me, "are the most intelligent and best-read. Their intelligence merely equips them to be meaner."

One day at Bobby Van's saloon we were interviewing each
other on a tiny tape recorder at the request of some Southern
papers. It was a Sunday afternoon of an incomparable autumn
and we were watching a football game and talking during the
lulls in the action.

If it hadn't have been for that war, I'd have found
something else to write about, I guess. That war just
happened to have come along at a certain time in my
life. My works really are a sort of personal odyssey.
If there hadn't been any war at all, I'd have written

about something else that happened to me. The Korean War and Vietnam War are not my subjects at all, really, because I had no serious, personal involvement in either one. So, because I was involved as a young man in World War II, it was a portion of the odyssey I'm making on earth, on the planet, as an individual person . . .

I don't consider writing a competitive sport, and I never have. I think that when fine writers reach a certain level of excellence, the idea that one of them is better than another ceases to matter. I've always felt this about any generation of writers, and if they're playing games like that, it's only personal vanity, which at my age I can no longer afford.

Someone once asked Sammy Reshevsky, the chess master, what he did with his spare time. He's a CPA by profession; he never made enough money at chess to live off it. And he's a very vain and arrogant man, Mr. Reshevsky. He looked at the man and he said, "Well, I don't know. I just kind of stay home and I read a lot of chess books, and other books." And the interviewer said, "Well, Mr. Reshevsky, do you go around, do you have a lot of other chess masters who are your friends?" And Reshevsky said, "My God, no. As a group, chess masters are the most conniving, evil, backbiting, knife-stabbing sonsabitches that I've ever seen in my life."

And this seems to be true of some writers, which shouldn't be. Maybe with chess masters, you have to have that kind of aggressiveness. But writers don't sit down at a board and gibe each other over a novel and say checkmate and bishop to king four, or whatever. I don't think it's the same kind of thing. That kind of jealousy and egomania, I think, is detrimental

216

finally to a man's work in the end. I think it damaged
Hemingway a great deal, and I think it damaged
Scott Fitzgerald a great deal.

The day Saul Bellow was awarded the Nobel Prize, I remember Jim saying: "I'm happy for him. I admire him. It's
good for American literature."

Wherever possible, he tried to help young writers avoid
some of the pitfalls he himself had suffered. He was generous with his time to unpublished writers. Winston Groom,
a reporter with the Washington *Star,* had quit his job to
write a combat novel set in Vietnam, where he had been as
an infantry lieutenant fresh out of the University of Alabama
and survived its bitterest fighting. The novel would be called
Better Times Than These. He had met Jim several months
before in Washington and then with his severance pay moved
out to Long Island to write the book. He remembered: "I
was floundering and flailing in a void, grappling with all
these made-up ideas and wondering if they were any good
at all." It was a cold winter, the book had not been sold, and
he was running out of money:

> Jim had taken immediate interest in the book. The
> first time we talked about it he thought over the brief
> story line I told him and handed out the following
> advice: "Whoever this main character of yours is, I
> think you should make him as different from yourself
> as possible. There'll be enough similarities anyway,
> but I'd make him different so far as background and
> looks and everything else." On many other occasions
> after I moved to Long Island, he would always ask
> about the book. He wanted to know about the char-

acters and what was going on. He asked to see a copy of the first hundred pages and after he'd read them he called up and asked me to come over. We sat around that big kitchen table one afternoon, just the two of us. "I'm going to show you a few things," he said. We spent an hour, or maybe more, going over some pages. They were subtle, marvelous techniques he'd learned over the years. "If you lop off this sentence and make it a separate paragraph here, it gives a punch to the scene," he'd say. Or, "Instead of having this character tell this part of the story, just take his best quotes and use them and tell the rest in third person. It saves half the space." He said: "One of the hardest things to do is to show something about one character by having another character think about what the first character is thinking or might be thinking. I'm trying to do that now, in *Whistle,* and I ain't done it before. But it's a damned good device." We had a couple of those sessions and each time I came away with something I didn't know before.

Dick Weber, a professor of English at Southampton College, asked Jim if he would come speak to the students:

He talked to an overflow crowd about his life as a writer. He fought off an attack of breathlessness that night to share himself with us. He answered questions, both the intelligent and the foolish, with an equanimity that astonished me. In my naïveté, I suppose I expected him to mix the stoicism of Prewitt with the explosive expletives of Milton Anthony Warden.

The next summer he appeared at our college

writers' conference. He radiated serene self-posses-
sion. He emerged as a human being who, through
many difficult experiences and thoughtful wrestling
with them, had stripped himself to the bare bones of
his being. Between comments about writing and an-
swering questions, he read a selection from *Whistle*.
As he stood in the morning sunlight, his words
created the picture of a small group of men whose
shared wartime experiences had annealed their relationship into a brotherhood. After months of separa-
tion, the survivors were being reunited at a base hospital. Those already there, waiting for the others, felt
sadness beyond grief, and an acceptance of their
lives together. As he read to us that morning, I felt
the same way about him. He was somewhere else, a
wisdom place, and it was fine being there.

14.

The days passed—another summer and autumn into winter, and Christmas approached again.

He was having trouble breathing, sudden attacks of breathlessness which came without warning. He made an appointment with his heart specialist in Huntington, a large commuter city halfway down the Island toward New York where Walt Whitman had once lived. He did not want Gloria to go; he asked me to drive down with him.

When we got there, he went through a series of tests which lasted nearly two hours. Then he came out into the waiting room. The doctor had told him his lungs were filling again and that his heart was seriously enlarged. The doctor had reserved a bed in the hospital and told him to check in right away.

We got in the car and drove down a steep hill toward the

hospital. The streets at noontime were festive wih Christmas decorations, and flurries of snow swept by in the wind.

"He told me I can't drink no more, goddam it. Not if I want to live." He said it faintly, with resignation.

We were driving by a huge restaurant and bar called Glynn's Inn. "Let's go in that place!" he suddenly exclaimed. "The hospital can wait. Fuck the hospital. I want to have two or three drinks."

"Are you sure?"

"Yeah. My last ones."

The bar was dark and deserted at this hour. There was Christmas music on the Muzak, and the dining room next door bustled with the chatter of commuters' wives at their lunches. Walt Whitman was a long way from here. We sat down at the bar and ordered a bottle of white wine. He took a sip and said: "What I'd give for a big-assed tumbler of scotch."

It was hard for him to give up drinking. In Europe, and in the years before, he was known as a sound drinker—a man's drinker. His work was filled with all the nuances of booze, the glories and miseries, the highs and lows of it. Not too long before, sitting around the kitchen table in Sagaponack, I had read in a chapter of *Whistle* about Top Sergeant Winch:

> "You're just going to have to get used to the idea that you can never take one drink again for the rest of your life," the doctor said.
> "I'm used to it," Winch said.
> But he wasn't. When he thought about it, it was enough to have him almost biting the walls. It was astonishing, when you got down to it and noticed it, how much almost everything in America had to do

with drinking. Every dinner. Every meal. Almost every social occasion. If you were chasing some girl. And at night, when everybody was philosophizing about life and the war and death, or dancing and trying to make out with some broad, if you did not drink you were outside everything. And bored to death by all of it.

We sat in the darkened bar talking about such things, about how a man's life changes, about the inevitability of sorrow, about death.

"I watched ol' Bill Styron once. We used to go around in Paris and raise hell. One afternoon we were in a mood to celebrate. I don't remember what over. We were sitting in a bar and I decided to keep count. I'd never done that before with my buddy Bill. I noticed for every three drinks I had, Bill only had one. It was the first time I ever saw how he paced himself. I couldn't do that. It disturbed me I couldn't, but I didn't really give a shit."

He lit a cigar and sipped on the wine. "It was hard enough when I realized I couldn't fight no more," he said. "Fight some son-of-a-bitch who was acting mean or trying to make out with my wife. Not doing that no more puts a whole new light on things."

I wanted to know if he really hit that guy over the head with the pinball machine in Europe.

"Yeah, I guess so. There were two of them. Trying to molest Gloria in a bar called Jerry Cherchio's in Rome."

The Christmas tunes wafted out from the music machine. The bartender poured another wine.

"Hell, Kaylie was asking me about death the other day. I told her life is a great adventure, and death is one of those adventures. I advised her to try and look at it that way. That's hard for a kid, though. They don't know much of nothing. They have to learn it all themselves. It's good they don't really feel about death. They *have* to be self-centered little creatures. Shit, otherwise the young wouldn't survive. I guess we have to take care of them for a while, though.

"I guess about the worst I ever saw of it was on the burial details. The graves-registration officer would come by and ask for three or four men out of the company, and the first sergeant would pick them. Once we were out digging up these temporary graves—that was the time this boy from the company found his brother in one of them. We always laughed a lot to keep, you know, from cracking."

He looked down into his wine. I said it was about time to get to the hospital. He downed the glass. "Well, that's that," he said. We went outside in the snow and drove to the hospital. He was there for two weeks on that trip, and got out on Christmas Eve, just in time for the big tree at Chateau Spud.

15.

That February I went to Washington for a couple of months to be writer-in-residence on the Washington *Star*. Jim wanted a break from his book, and he brought down his son Jamie and my son David, who were both then fifteen, for a two-week visit. They stayed at a hotel in Old Town in Alexandria, just around the corner from my apartment. We planned eventually to take our sons through some of the Civil War country.

The day after they got there was Washington's Birthday, and since it was the bicentennial year and Alexandria was Washington's hometown, there was an enormous parade through the old, narrow streets of the city, which was splendidly bedecked in national streamers for the occasion. The parade was made up of high school bands, floats, crack platoons from the military schools, girl scouts, volunteer firemen, not to mention the best military bands from the District.

the group, proper and reverential foreigners. We were walking through the Rose Garden on the way to the Oval Office. It was so early in the day that President Ford was not there yet.

Suddenly, in the Rose Garden, Jim dropped behind the group. He was bent over examining something. Winston Groom asked him what was wrong. "Look at this," he said. "I got some fucking dog shit all over my shoe. It must be Ford's damned old dog." The dog shit was all over the heel of his shoe, and up on the sides. He picked up some leaves and tried to rub it off, then reached in his satchel and brought out a knife to scrape with. "I can't go into the Oval Office and track dog shit on the carpet," he said. "This sort of thing is always happening to me." Finally we went into the room, bathed in its preternatural quiet, and lingered there a few minutes while the guide pointed out the President's desk, and the Stuart portrait of Washington, and the holes in the floor made by Eisenhower's golf spikes. "I hate doing something like that," he said a little later. "Did you smell anything in there?"

We drove southwest into Virginia that week, into that haunted ground where the toll of death had been so monumental. Visiting the battlefields between the Rapidan and the Rappahannock, he was haunted by the fact that the two massed armies in the spring of 1864 were fighting on the same terrain of battles of a year before, so that the men who had survived that year and come back again to Virginia saw the old scenes of devastation, the skeletons of men and horses, the burnt-out woods, the makeshift graves. "For this was the year when the shadow of death lay across America," Bruce Catton wrote, "and grotesque shapes moved within the shadows and laid hold of men's minds and hearts." Wandering about these places—Chancellorsville, the Wilderness, Spotsylvania—sometimes startling the illicit couples in parked cars who find their privacy in battlefields on winter afternoons—we talked a lot about what coming back to all this must have meant to the soldiers.

He was a close student of the Civil War, not just of the tactics and strategy of it, but of the whole spiritual, mystical weight of it on our civilization. Once I had told him in some detail of my search, as a boy in Mississippi, for the battlefield of Champion's Hill, which was situated halfway between Vicksburg and Jackson. In the spring of 1863 there had been a bloody battle there, and as soon as I was old enough to drive, having learned the vast battlefield of Vicksburg with its thousands of graves almost by heart then, I went searching for the lesser battleground of Champion's Hill. I could never find anything to look at. The dead had been exhumed and moved to Vicksburg after the war, there were no monuments there, and the whole terrain had been allowed to grow over with vegetation—an eerie landscape where hundreds of American boys had died, right on American soil, and nothing there to show for it. My story had obsessed him. He went to his books and read all about Champion's Hill, and said he would go there someday.

At Chancellorsville that day he wanted to trace Stonewall Jackson's flanking movement against Hooker. At the Bloody Angle in the Wilderness he stood alone in the sunlight for a long time. He knew this land and what it meant. He sought out the area where Lee had come up close to the front lines but his men would not let him go any farther. He quoted what Lee said to Longstreet in the most terrible moments at Fredericksburg, when the Northern infantry was being cut to pieces by impregnable guns from the hills, and during the rebel countercharge at Deep Run: "It is well that war is so terrible—we should grow too fond of it."

I remembered 'Bama Dillert's words to Dave Hirsch while they were driving in their big black car through the South in *Some Came Running:*

> "I figure it was all sort of fate," 'Bama said. "Just fate," he said. "I don't think the United States was meant to be broken up into two little countries; where would we be today? against Russia? if we had? But you know," he said academically again, "there was only two real geniuses came out of the war, and that's Forrest and Jackson. There was a lot of great generals, but there was only those two real geniuses. Even old Lee wasn't a real genius I don't think. A great general, yes, but not a genius.
>
> "You know," he said, "I don't know whether I read it someplace or somebody told me or I thought it up myself, but I think it would be a fine thing if someday—when the very last two survivin' members of the Northern and Southern Armies finally died— they would plan to bury them together, in one grave at Arlington, and put one big monument over both of them. They could say something like: HERE, UNITED IN DEATH, LIE THE LAST TWO SURVIVIN' MEMBERS OF THE NORTHERN AND SOUTHERN ARMIES IN THE WAR OF 1865."

We drove on down to Charlottesville, where the next day we were going to see Monticello and the University of Virginia, through the courthouse towns, the facades of buildings in shadow and sunlight along their streets, with little boys everywhere shooting baskets in back yards. Late at night we checked into a Holiday Inn and took adjoining rooms with a connecting door and, as traveling Americans will do, turned on the television sets in each room as casually as one opens a window to get another view. In a few moments Jim came into David's and my room.

"Say, that column you did for the *Star* on us going to the Jefferson Memorial the other day—you know, the one you let me read? Is it too late to call the copy desk and make a small change?"

What did he want changed?

"Well, you said I went inside the Memorial smoking a cigar. I didn't do that. I put out the cigar before I went inside, in one of them little ashtrays on the side of the building. I wouldn't go inside there smoking a cigar. You know what I mean?"

Was it the same principle as not wishing to trail dog shit into the Oval Office? I telephoned the copy desk and got the sentence changed. "Thanks," he said. "It don't sound like much, but it's been worrying me like hell for two days."

In just such as this, he was an entertaining man to ride around the country with. The next day, heading west toward the Blue Ridge to loop about the Massanutten and aim toward Harpers Ferry and Antietam, we picked up some hamburgers and french fries at a roadside place and continued on our way. After a while he asked David, who was sitting in the front seat next to him, to reach down and hand him the french fries he had dropped a few miles back.

"They're under your foot," David said. "They've got dirt and mud all over them."

"I don't give a damn if the fleas from your ears got on them. I've eaten a lot worse in my day, and I hope you boys don't never have to. Now reach down and get me my french fries like I asked you. And get in the back seat if you're shocked."

In gathering mists we drove toward Harpers Ferry, the Potomac and the Shenandoah appearing suddenly as if from nowhere in their eternal twistings and turnings. We sped by a road sign. "How many miles did that sign say to Harpers Ferry?" he asked.

"Six," I said.

"I thought so, too."

From the back seat Jamie and David both demurred. "It said twenty-six," they argued.

"It said six."

"It said twenty-six."

We drove on, considerably more than six miles. From the back seat was the sound of whispers and laughter. Finally, after about twenty-six miles, we reached the outskirts of Harpers Ferry.

"We told you it wasn't six," a voice came from the back.

"I knew you'd say that," Jim said. "All I been doing is waiting on it. I'd advise you to look at it this way. It's the first thing you two assholes have said in a week that made any sense."

Antietam is a place linked closely to the Federal City seventy miles away. Washington might be a different concept altogether if that fortuitous clash of two great armies on September 17, 1862, had taken a different turn, and so also, of course, might the nation. It was a draw, if such things can be called that, but it meant Lee had to call off his invasion of the North and return to Virginia; it also meant three more years of war. It enabled Lincoln to issue his preliminary Emancipation Proclamation.

It was the bloodiest single day's fighting in the Civil War, some say the bloodiest in the history of mankind up to then. The men on both sides were caught in outdated formations by the fire of deadly weaponry, new and old. They fell in rows. At Antietam, Jim remembered, they were firing cannon with chain shot almost point-blank, two cannonballs attached with a long chain, and when fired the chain would extend and cut men in half. More than 23,000 Americans fell that day; 6,600 fell on D day in France.

We paused for a long time at the Dunker Church. It was a day of mists and unhurried rain, and there was an ominous rumble way off toward the skyline; it sounded very much like artillery. Was it A. P. Hill and his brigades back to try again?

The ironies and juxtapositions were a little insane. The federal government owned only strips and fragments of the land where the fighting took place, so all about us were farmhouses and even trailer houses with long television aerials and abandoned cars in back right next to some spot where hundreds of men died. Cows grazed in fields which had run with blood, chickens and dogs went about their pleasures, and the farmers had planted corn in those places where men were knocked out of the ranks by the dozens. Far out in one cornfield, separated from us by the wire fence marking that this was the end of federal property, there was a lonely monument with a lion on top, with corn furrows going around it on each side. This, Jim and I surmised from our maps, was where Sedgwick's men were ambushed by Stonewall Jackson. I told Jim it reminded me of Tennyson's poem:

> The woods decay, the woods decay and fall,
> The vapors weep their burthens to the ground,
> Man comes and tills the fields and lies beneath,
> And after many a summer dies the swan.

At the observation point in the West Woods we talked about the strategy, Lee with 40,000 men, McClellan with

90,000, how Lee continually moved men from one place to another against the odds. "Did you see that picture of Lee in the museum?" he said. "It's the one that shows that beneath the sweet, benign, religious facade, he was a very tough man. He knew that if you're a soldier settled into the mire, you don't know what's going on all around you. You got no notion of the whole picture. It's hard enough for the generals. They don't know themselves a lot of the time. Lee knew a hell of a lot more than the others, and this is a perfect example right here."

Jim wore a slouch hat and walking boots and tarried in the cold wind with a pair of binoculars. It was melancholy land with its hollows and ravines and outcroppings which snipers used, and they could hide a whole brigade in some of those places. "It was a damned general's paradise," he said, as he peered through the binoculars at the ground where Stonewall Jackson hid his men, "but very hard on the legs of the troops. One of the things most people don't understand is the physical hardship a soldier goes through even when he's not being shot at. The average person couldn't climb that hill at Burnside's Bridge just to get there. And going downhill is sometimes even more draining than going uphill. If you've been a soldier you look at all that, I guess."

"If we'd been living then and been here, we'd probably have fought against each other," I said.

"Yeah. I guess that's true."

The day waned on in its fog and rain, and we worked our way from Nicodemus Hill down the Smoketown Lane and past the Roulette Farmhouse, and now we were at the Sunken Road, which at the time became known as Bloody Lane. Here, along a line of a thousand yards, the Confederate center took its stand, thousands of them firing at close quarters against the

Federal troops charging across the crest of a ridge. It lasted three hours, and the dead Confederate soldiers lay so thick here that as far as the eye could see a man could walk upon them without once touching ground, and the bodies of the attackers lay strewn in piles across the whole ridge.

We walked down the road for a while, and gazed out every so often from behind the wooden fences at the crest where the attackers came. Our two boys were quiet now also, and for a moment they looked silently at the monument only a few feet to the south of the road, dedicated to an Ohio brigade, and at the top of this was the stone silhouette of a boy who seemed to be no more than eighteen, raising his cap in one hand, holding a flag in the other. To the right of the Sunken Road was an observation tower, evil-smelling with the reek of urine. We climbed to the top of it. The view from here was spectacular, the blue mountains at the horizon, the sweeping sky, the landscape below in the mist, the Sunken Road itself sweeping almost to the opposite skyline.

"The way men go to die," Jim said, looking down at the ridge before us. "It's incredibly sad. It breaks my heart. You wonder why it was necessary, why human beings have to do that to each other. This reminds me a little of Europe, where every blade of grass has twenty-one drops of human blood on it. That's why Europe's so goddamned green."

Why do men do it, one of the boys wondered. Why did they do it here?

"Well . . ." He paused, to the sound of rain on the roof. "I think it's more because they didn't want to appear unmanly in front of their friends. On the average I think that counted more than anything. Men don't like to be shot at. Take my word for it. They'd rather have been anywhere else than here. If you could just get men to expend the courage and energy on things that weren't destructive to other men, what a race we'd be. What was it Steinbeck said? Man has conquered every natural obstacle in the world except himself."

But the average run-of-the-mill of human experience is so full of sorrow and brutality anyway, I said.

"Without war," he said. "Yeah. You and I know that. We're writers. I honestly think people in a way want war to escape the ordinary sorrow we have to deal with. I honestly believe that. But these men would've had to be mystical to go farther than they did. I don't think men could go any farther than these men did in this battle and still be members of the planet."

We descended the tower, and the boys and I walked to our car. Jim had dallied somewhere, however, and I went looking for him. He was a solitary figure in a slouch hat, standing there in the middle of the Sunken Road. It was early afternoon, and we drove back to the motel in Harpers Ferry. I had to write an article and telephone it in to Washington, and the boys went down to the village to take a tour. Jim went back to the battlefield in the rain and stayed until dark. He returned to the motel room soaking wet.

"Why did you go back in this weather?" I asked.

"I don't know," he said. "I guess you really have to be alone in a place like that."

On the drive back to Washington that night, we decided that the four of us would make another trip someday soon: first to Robinson, Illinois, which he had not been back to since '57, and then through Kentucky and Tennessee. We would stop in Memphis to look for whatever landmarks remained of his days there, in the hospital in '43 and later in the trailer camp when he was working on *From Here to Eternity*—then on down to Yazoo City, Mississippi. It was a trip we never made.

16.

By the following January, he was well into the last of the five main books of *Whistle,* called "The End of It." Then the night came when we had to get him to the hospital in Southampton in the blizzard, Gloria and I following the ambulance down the Montauk Highway, going slow as could be to avoid skidding off the road into snowdrifts. They almost lost his pulse in the ambulance.

"There ain't nothing wrong with my old heart," he said in the bed in the Cardiac Care Unit. "I got a good heart." For two or three days we thought he was dying. He asked me to get a notebook. The doctors left us alone for a long time. I sat by the bed and between whiffs on the oxygen mask he talked about the few remaining chapters of his novel.

He survived that attack, but he was extremely weak. When he got out of the hospital in February, the doctors warned him not to work at first. But gradually he started back into the hard routine.

It was a malevolent winter, that winter of '77. It was the cruelest winter in years on Long Island, and it was killing him. All around, the countryside was deep in snow, the bare branches heavy with ice, crackling in the gusts of wind. Every little bump in the road seemed to get after you. The flat fields stretching toward the ocean filled one with a wrenching desolation. Children skated in the low places in the fields, and here and there, under the bleak skies, a solitary farmer would be surveying his terrain. That winter he learned that his brother Jeff, whom he had not seen in a long time, died of congestive heart failure in Roanoke at the age of sixty-seven.

At nights around the kitchen table we would sometimes go over the notes on his few remaining chapters. Our friend Joe Heller had given him a small tape recorder, and as a precaution he was also talking some into that. Mainly he was trying to conserve his strength to get in a few hours a day at the writing desk. Then he would start coming out again, and he would be with Gloria at the bar at Bobby Van's at lunchtime as before, drinking grapefruit juice on the rocks, smoking cigars, and talking with people.

Maria Koenig and Peter Matthiessen made a big dinner for him at their house near the ocean in Sagaponack one evening that winter—oysters on the half shell and pepper steak to suit his diet. "I'd known Jim for twenty years," Peter said, "but never saw him much except in crowds until he came to live in Sagaponack, and even then we led different kinds of lives. Yet I knew we agreed on mortal matters that were hard to speak about, and he knew it, too, and perhaps what lay at the heart of this shy friendship was this instinct that we had something to tell each other when the time came. It never did." But that evening after dinner Jim told them of the vivid image he had

had when he came so close to death in the hospital that January. He and Gloria had owned a little French vegetable-steaming machine in Paris, a circular gadget with brass panels which opened and closed. His vision was that he was in the center of this machine, fighting for his last breath, and he knew that when the last panel clicked and closed upon him, it would be all over. Then there was this dramatic clicking again, and the panels started opening around him, freeing him; only when they opened did he know he had made it. He described this in minute detail, and Peter had the feeling he had worked it out carefully in his mind, as if he would use it in a book someday.

Around the table after dinner in his house he talked one night to me about a scene he was looking forward to writing, and which was all in his head. Sergeant Winch takes his girl Carol to dinner in the staid, family-type restaurant of the Peabody Hotel in Memphis, or Luxor. What ensues is a sign both of Winch's suffering from his heart ailment and his increasing craziness. While in conversation at the dinner table with Carol, surrounded by the quiet, respectable citizens of Luxor, Winch lets loose this loud rippling fart which reverberates from the walls of the restaurant. There is a pronounced though short silence all over the place, a discreet turning of heads, and then the people at the other tables go back to their dinners. Winch continues talking as though nothing has happened, and so too does Carol. What else can she do? As Jim described this scene to me in its details, he started laughing. "I know it's supposed to be sad," he said, "but shit it's funny," and he put his head in his hands and laughed some more.

That got me to laughing too, uncontrollable laughter from the belly muscles, and to punctuate all this Jim at that moment farted, and we both damned near fell out of our chairs.

One day, just in case, he wrote down his dedication and showed it to us, something he said he had been turning over in his mind:

> This book is dedicated to every man who served in the U. S. Armed Forces in World War II—whether he survived or not, whether he made a fortune serving, or not; whether he fought or not; whether he did time or not; whether he went crazy, or didn't.

At other times he read to Gloria and me from a chapter he had just finished about Sergeant Landers' going AWOL in a little town in western Tennessee called Barleyville, where the sheriff puts him up and he gets to know the country people and sleeps with the sheriff's pregnant daughter Loucine. And some uproarious paragraphs about Sergeant Strange going out into the countryside on maneuvers. And then the chapter in which Landers makes his final, tragic return to Camp O'Bruyerre. I remember when he brought down the final paragraphs of that chapter for me to read. He said he wanted them to be right. Landers steps into the road and sees the woman behind the wheel of the car. He hears the wild squeal of the brakes. And perhaps a cry. And then the crash of glass. And a loud thumping thud.

> He saw or thought he saw the look of horror that came across her face in back of the windshield. Because she thought she was doing something wrong, and he wanted to laugh. The mouth a wildly spread O of lipstick. Eyebrows arched up. Eyes staring. He

hated to do all that to her. But, by God, at least she knew she had hit something. Then the helicopter moved away from the ship.

The big red crosses were still on its white flank. And the sea still moved backward along its waterline. Everything was still silence.

Far off, the great blue continent still stood. Uninhabited. Green with the silent, unpeopled forests and soft grasses. The breakers clashing on the white, unpeopled sands. And the silence of home.

Another night we were thumbing through the whole manuscript of what he had completed until then. He read from his last chapters. Then he read a few paragraphs about Bobby Prell's fight to save his legs. And then the paragraphs about Winch's going to see Top Sergeant Alexander in Luxor to enlist his help in saving Prell's legs:

. . . Winch had never served with Alexander and didn't know him . . . Alexander the Great—"The Emperor"—was just finishing his reign and shipping home with his loot he'd collected as number-one fighter in the Department, when Winch was just arriving in Wahoo as a lowly corporal. Alexander had been a legend in the Army, even then.

Now he was old. And he looked it. In fact, he resembled nothing so much as a huge, ancient, baitwise old sea turtle. With his totally bald head and thick-wrinkled face, his only slightly flattened beak and big jaw and lipless mouth like a razor blade, bleak as the edge of an ice floe. With his faded, pale, flat, blue eyes which had seen just about everything the earth had to offer, and neither liked nor hated it all that much. An old turtle who had swum the

oceans of his planet for two centuries, avoiding the
traps laid by men and wearing the scars to prove it,
until now he was so huge there wasn't anything for
him to fear any more.

Jim wiped a tear away—then smiled about it, and laughed at
himself for it.

I was so saddened by his physical condition. As the days
passed he became more thin and pale. In his farmhouse there
were times I went into the bathroom to fight back the tears.

Their old friends Clem and Jessie Wood came from Europe
to see them in March. He and Clem sat on the sofa by the fireplace one night and talked for a long time. "Jim always occupied a large cube of space," Clem remembered. "Now he was
delicate, almost transparent. 'I can only work a little a day,'
he said, 'but it's comin', it's comin'.' That last time I saw him,
when he talked to me about finishing *Whistle,* he suddenly
seemed an ascetic, a saint."

Robert Alan Aurthur—"Bob"—was Jim's good friend. He
lived a few miles away in The Springs and was in on the
poker games. He remembers the last one they played:

> The Old Sarge, Jim, played a classic game of
> enlisted man's poker. Deliberate, cool, covert;
> gnarled hands caressing a yet unseen draw as if faith
> and love could by some magic mix a busted hand
> into a winner. Unlike Gloria, who always sat to his
> right, and who cursed and moaned in defeat, jeered
> in victory, Jim was ever gracious, grumpy only when
> a rule of Hoyle went unobserved or when Gloria,
> generally twice a night, would bet into an open pair
> and be slaughtered. Even into *his* open pair. "Dumb
> broad," he'd mutter. "She'll *never* learn."

For two years in Sagaponack we played nearly every Tuesday in a room, set up for games, that was characterized by windows that wouldn't open and dominated by a garish full-figure portrait of their friend Jean Genet, brought from Paris, painted by a black American expatriate whom the Joneses supported with commissions. Through a common wall rock 'n' roll would boom from the hi-fi in Kaylie's bedroom, throbbing counterrhythm to the click of the unique Hermès chips: ivory slabs of many shapes and mysterious denominations. The first hand was dealt at eight, the last timed by an unvoiced group assessment of Jim's condition. As months passed and Jim grew visibly paler and more exhausted, the game ended earlier each week. But the bawdy jokes, the mock insults, the laughter never diminished.

Jamie, sixteen, was also a regular. Seated across the table from his father Jamie was a mirror image of Jim, learning the enlisted man's game. "He'd damn well better learn," Jim said repeatedly. "It's the only way he'll be able to earn his way through college." Then an old soldier's smile for his favorite recruit. The kid'll make it.

We played *real* poker; Jim would have no truck with those funny-name games. Serious poker. At first, quarter ante, pot limit, table stakes; but when too much money was lost by some the ante was cut to a dime.

Ten days before Jim went to the hospital for the last time we played what proved to be the final round. A hand of seven-card stud, and by the sixth card there are just two players left, Jim and Jamie. Both hands well disguised, both men extremely wary. The last down card. Cool and unhesitating Jim bets ten dollars. A moment passes; Jamie sees the

ten, raises twenty. Jim hunches over his hand, bale-
fully looks at his son through slitted eyes. Over the
silence, in mock awe, someone says: "The classic
Freudian drama. Father and son alone in the pit, son
determined to kill the father, the old man desperately struggling to hold him off."

Jim grins and slides in twenty dollars' worth of
Hermès ivory. "Wrong," he says, exposing a king-
high heart flush. "Father triumphant over asshole
kid."

Just the slightest smile from Jamie, who spread his
hand for all to see. "Spade flush, ace high," he says,
then rakes in the nearly hundred-dollar pot. Gloria
laughs, blows Jamie a kiss. The game is over. Jim
looks rueful. "Christ," he says, "that's not the way it's
supposed to come out."

One night in early April, not long before my mother died in
Mississippi, Gloria and the kids were making dinner in the
kitchen. He and I were sitting by the fireplace, talking about
nothing in particular. A silence fell.

I looked across the room at the ancient pulpit-bar, brought
back from the Île St. Louis to sit in this house in the fields of
Long Island. It was almost as if I could hear the old laughter
from Paris around it, the lost American voices, the clinking of
glasses, someone "invoking the pulpit," James Baldwin
preaching from behind it on the evils of drink, the sounds
from the Seine outside.

Suddenly, he said: "Goddam I love you, Willie. You're my
best friend."

After the longest moment I said: "I love you too. You're the
best friend I ever had."

I told him there were two wonderful old men down in Austin, Texas, when I was living there, two writers named Dobie and Bedichek who had known each other for years. Once Bedichek came up to Dobie at a party and said, "Dobie, you're good as grass," and Dobie said, "Bedi, you're fine as rain."

17.

On my long solitary journey in the car from Mississippi I had dwelled on all these many things—what I had learned of his life before I knew him, and these old mementos of a friendship . . .

I spent the last night on the road somewhere in Pennsylvania, and telephoned the hospital in Southampton to find he was sinking fast. Before dawn that morning I went through New Jersey toward the Long Island Expressway.

I drove into Southampton early on a Thursday afternoon, and went straight to the hospital. Gloria was in the waiting room outside the Cardiac Care Unit, and Kaylie and Jamie, and a number of close friends. Gloria told me to go inside.

The heart unit consisted of eight rooms and a central area where the pulse and heartbeat of each patient was monitored.

Jim was lying in the bed, with wires in him for the monitors and the glucose. He took my hand.

"Gee. I'm sorry about your mom. Did you get to Shiloh?"

I told him he was right about western Tennessee, that it was pretty much the way he described it.

"Did you inherit anything?"

The family silver was in the trunk of the car, I said—a Plymouth with Yazoo County plates.

He grinned. I sat in a chair by the bed while one of the nurses gave him a shot. When she left, he said: "Listen to me. Go to Sandy Richardson, like I told you to. Write two books fairly quick, and then—da, da, da, da—the next ones will come."

He lay there for a moment, wordlessly, then reached for the oxygen mask.

"I'm scared, Willie."

"We'll stay with you, Jim. You're fine."

"Aw, shit, it ain't that. I'm scared I ain't finished *Whistle*."

"But you have really. You know that."

"Just them three short chapters. I never quite got to the fart scene in the Peabody. I been talking some more into this thing Joe Heller give me. I gave Gloria two more tapes while you were gone." The tape recorder was on the table by the bed. I sat there a few minutes until he fell asleep.

We remained in the waiting room all through the afternoon. Someone had hidden some bottles and paper cups under a sofa. Gloria told me that the night before our friend Jack Knowles had tried to console her; he had told her after they had all had some drinks that even if Jim died, a slightly unfinished book might be dramatic and even commercially advantageous, like *The Last Tycoon*, or the *Unfinished Symphony*, an effort at consolation which said something about

245

the affection and shameless candor of the community in which we lived. "Jack was trying to help me," she said. "Early this morning I went in and told Jim what Jack said. He didn't say anything, just drifted off to sleep for an hour, and when he woke up he looked at me with one cocked eye and said, "Tell Jack Knowles to go fuck off."

We sat there in the waiting room, huddled close together, as old friends will. Now, in the early evening, the doctor suddenly came out and took Gloria and the children aside. He told them it was just a matter of time, perhaps an hour. They went in again to see him.

In about an hour Gloria emerged. "Quick!" she said. "He wants a drink." I poured a paper cup full of bourbon. She hurried inside with it.

All that evening we waited; Gloria, Adam Shaw, and I took turns sleeping on the floor. The doctor later said he had practiced heart medicine for twenty years and had never seen a patient come back like that from the edge of death; he had never seen a patient want to live so much.

At 2 A.M. the nurse came out and said Jim wanted to see me. I went into his room. He was lying in bed. "I think I'm going to pack it in," he said. "I got to talk to you. But I got to get unhooked. I can't think with all this shit." He pulled out the wires, and got out of bed. He sat down in a chair and reached for the recorder. "Sit here next to me," he said. I sat on the floor by the chair.

"I want you to listen to this. I got to fill in two points I didn't make clear. They been bothering me. It'll be on this tape—the one in the machine now. Don't erase the damned thing by mistake. You got to help me out."

He began talking into the machine. He talked for a long time, weakly but lucidly. First he talked about the end of the

246

affair between Top Sergeant Winch and his girl from Memphis, Carol. Then, at greater length, he described precisely how Winch, in the next-to-last chapter, got the two hand grenades which he would use to blow up the Wurlitzer machines in the PX at Camp O'Bruyerre:

> Being a top sergeant and now a junior warrant officer, he was on friendly terms with the grenade officer and grenade warrant officer. He went down to the grenade range one afternoon and when no one was looking he casually picked up a couple of grenades and slipped one into each pocket of his coat. Later, in his room, he unscrewed them with a pair of pliers and poured the powder into a jar, which he hid. For two or three nights he slept with the defused grenades under his pillow . . .

He continued for a while, about how Winch's grenades blew up not only the Wurlitzers, but the whole PX as well. When he had finished he sat back exhausted. "Those were the two points I needed to clear up," he said. "God, I'm sleepy."

He deteriorated badly that weekend. Irwin Shaw flew in from Europe and rushed from the airport to the hospital. Gloria went in to tell Jim he was there.

"Tell Irwin our Jewish God don't have a sense of humor," he said.

In a little while the doctors let Irwin into the room. It was the last exchange between these two old comrades.

"You look worse than I do," Jim said.

"Sure, Jim," his friend replied. "You're not drinking."

Gloria was now with him most of the time. She came out later and said he wanted a copy of Yeats's *Lake Isle of*

Innisfree. She said he wanted it read at his service. It was Sunday afternoon, and everyone went home to rest.

David and I drove to Bridgehampton and got the poem. We returned to the hospital and went to his room.

"Only a few minutes," the nurse warned.

I handed him the poem. He lifted his hand high to avoid entangling it in the wires, and read it to himself.

"It's a strange poem," he said finally. "It has to be read in a certain way—a certain rhythm on the last line of each stanza." He paused.

"It makes me want to weep." He fought back at the tears with a sweep of his hand.

Slowly, in the old familiar gruff voice, he read it aloud.

> I will arise and go now, and go to
> Innisfree,
>   And a small cabin build there, of clay
> and wattles made;
>   Nine bean rows will I have there, a hive
> for the honey bee,
>   And live alone in the bee-loud glade.
>
>   And I shall have some peace there, for
> peace comes dropping slow,
>   Dropping from the veils of the morning to
> where the cricket sings;
>   There midnights's all a-glimmer, and noon
> a purple glow,
>   And evening full of the linnet's wings.
>
> I will arise and go now, for always night and day
> I hear lake water lapping with low sounds by
> the shore;
>   While I stand on the roadway, or on the pavements
> gray,
>   I hear it in the deep heart's core.

The nurse came in and told us to go. David left, and I stood briefly in the doorway.

"I'll see you tomorrow, ol' Jim."

"I'll see you, ol' buddy."

But soon he lapsed into a coma. Gloria and the children were with him all that next afternoon. Early Monday evening he struggled to get out of the bed, and then he died.

After a succession of beautiful days, a Long Island storm had been gathering that afternoon. Thunder and lightning filled the skies. By nightfall the trees from the windows of the hospital swayed in the ocean wind, and it began to rain in torrents.

Everyone suddenly left for home. In the heart unit the nurses were crying. Peter Matthiessen and I waited for the undertaker. He arrived shortly with the forms to be filled out. We retired to the waiting room.

He asked the first question. "Was Mr. Jones a veteran?"

Peter and I looked at each other. "Yes," I said. "He was."

18.

In front of the Bridgehampton Library, in a display case, they put a photograph of him smoking a cigar, along with the hand-lettered words: *"From Here to Eternity . . ."*

Rose Styron was in Paris. She heard the news on the French radio.

> I walked over to the house on the île. I had to be there. I stood outside the house. Only then did I realize that he didn't live there any more, that I hadn't the faintest notion who was living there. I sat alone on the wall of the bridge where we used to sit. I looked up at our balcony. Everything was in bloom; Paris was gorgeous. Nothing had changed, and everything had.

In Hawaii his death was marked by the publication on the front page of the Honolulu *Star-Bulletin* of a long excerpt from his *Viet Journal*, in the last part of which he wrote about returning to Honolulu in 1973, looking for the landmarks he had remembered in *From Here to Eternity*.

I myself remembered what Faulkner had said, that the great writer himself "partakes of the immortality which he has engendered."

> Someday he will be no more, which will not matter then, because isolated and itself invulnerable, [the written word] remains that which is capable of engendering still the old deathless excitement of hearts and glands whose owners and custodians are generations from even the air he breathed and anguished in; if it was capable once, he knows that it will be capable and potent still long after there remains of him only a dead and fading name.

Shortly after his death, Joan Didion made a spiritual odyssey from the mainland to Honolulu. She would write about it in *Esquire*.

> Certain places seem to exist mainly because someone had written about them. Kilimanjaro belongs to Ernest Hemingway. Oxford, Mississippi, belongs to William Faulkner, and one hot July week in Oxford I was moved to spend an afternoon walking the graveyard looking for his stone, a kind of courtesy call on the owner of the property. A place belongs forever to whoever claims it hardest, remembers it most obsessively, wrenches it from itself, shapes it, renders it, loves it so radically that he remakes it in his image, and not only Schofield Barracks but a great deal of Honolulu itself has always belonged for me to James Jones.

She made the trip for the same reason she had walked the Mississippi graveyard—a courtesy call of love on the owner. The men she met at Schofield in their green fatigues all knew exactly who James Jones was and what he had written and even where he had slept and eaten and gotten drunk during his years there. They anticipated the places she would want to see: D Quad, the old stockade, Hotel Street, Kole Kole Pass.

> James Jones had known a great simple truth: the Army was nothing more or less than life itself. I wish I could tell you that on the day in May when James Jones died someone had played taps for him at Schofield Barracks, but I think this is not the way life goes.

There was taps for him, however, at the memorial service in the Bridgehampton Community House. When we requested a bugler from Washington, we asked for an enlisted man who was also a career soldier. An officer in the Department of the Army telephoned shortly: They had a career soldier, he said, but he was not an enlisted man. "All the best buglers these days are master sergeants," he explained.

"Then just so he's a good bugler," someone said.

"Our man is not only the best damned bugler in the U. S. Army. He's the best bugler in the world. He's played at the graves of three Presidents. And he volunteered for this assignment. He's right here."

Master Sergeant Patrick Mastroleo came on the line. He admired Mr. Jones, he said—he remembered Montgomery Clift in *From Here to Eternity*.

Now, on that afternoon of high spring, someone read the

252

scene from the novel, and the sergeant in his dress blues sounded taps firm and clear, as Prewitt had at Schofield many years before.

The apple blossoms and lilacs were in bloom on the morning we buried his ashes. Bill Styron came to fetch me at the back window of my house just as Jim had always done; for an instant I thought it was Jim shouting to get me up, so we could go somewhere and hang around. There was just a small group of us in the old cemetery down the road from his farmhouse. Bill read a poem:

> . . . or set upon a golden bough to sing
> To lords and ladies of Byzantium
> Of what is past, or passing, or to come.

Irwin Shaw said, "Goodbye, Jim. The adventure is over," and that was all. The gravestone is there now, set in a far corner of the clipped greensward: "James Jones: 1921–1977." The veterans put a flag on it on Memorial Day, as they did on the graves of the soldiers of the Revolutionary War buried there with him.

We transcribed his tapes, and I sat at his worktable in the attic and put together his notes for the last three chapters.

Several hours before he died, alone in his hospital room, he had recited to himself on the last bit of tape *The Lake Isle of Innisfree*.

President Carter wrote Gloria: "The death of James Jones deprives us of a writer whose work illuminated the most profound collective experience of his generation, the experience of war."

That war, World War II, was indeed a *world* war, one of the memorable events of mankind, more catastrophic perhaps than anything in the history of the human race. Hundreds upon hundreds of thousands of men and women were swept up in it, consumed by it, on both sides. It is a compelling thought to ponder that this boy from Robinson, Illinois, from all the countries, is the one person to have given us this stunning corpus of work which will be read and remembered and reread five hundred years from now.

I remember one night two years before when he came down from the attic with some pages he had just written for *Whistle*. They were about a bad fight in a hotel bar of the city where the Army hospital was located; two members of the old company have beaten up several Navy men who were trying to take an empty chair. One of them, Sergeant Landers, kept yelling *Pay!* every time he swung his fists. Later, in the hotel room, one of the local girls asked him why he had shouted Pay. The paragraphs which followed were Landers' response.

"I don't know whether I should keep these paragraphs in," he had said that night. "Maybe they're too spelt out. They hurt a lot. I'll have to think about it some more."

"What did you mean?" Annie Waterfield asked him, "when you kept hollerin' Pay?"

"Hollering Pay?" Landers said. "Pay?"

"Yes. Every time you hit somebody you kept hollerin' 'Pay! Pay, you sons of bitches! Pay, pay, pay!'"

"I don't know," Landers said hollowly. "I don't remember saying that. I don't know what I meant."

But he thought he did know. It was easy to say it was because of the booze they had put away. But

Landers knew there was something more. There was something in him aching to get out, but in a way that only a serious fight or series of serious fights would let it get out. Anguish. Love. And hate . . .

There was no way on earth to explain it to anybody, though. Not without sounding shitty. There was no way to say it . . .

Landers thought that, probably, it had been building in him. Growing. Ever since he was sitting on that damned evil hilltop in New Georgia, with all those other weeping men with the white streaks down their dirty faces, watching the men below in the valley whanging and beating and shooting and killing each other, with such stern, disruptive, concentrated effort.

Anguish. Love. And hate . . . The anguish was for himself. And every poor slob like him, who had ever suffered fear, and terror, and injury at the hands of other men. The love, he didn't know who the love was for. For himself and everybody. For all the sad members of this flawed, misbegotten, miscreated race of valuable creatures, which was trying and failing with such ruptured effort to haul itself up out of the mud and dross and drouth of its crippled heritage. And the hate, implacable, unyielding, was for himself and every other who had ever, in the name of whatever good, maimed or injured or killed another man . . .

He kept them in.

Acknowledgments

Many of the quotations and episodes in this book came out of my talks and experiences with James Jones over the years, and after his death, from conversations with his wife Gloria. I see no need to cite them as sources page by page, since these sections more or less speak for themselves.

I'm grateful to the following people for their recollections, given to me in letters or conversations or both:

Robert Alan Aurthur, quoted on pp. 240, 241, and 242.
Cecile Gray Bazelon—pp. 88, 89, 90, 91, and 199.
Bill Belli—pp. 191 and 192.
Eugene Braun-Munk—pp. 104, 105, 123, 141, 142, 147, and 157.
Ross Claiborne—pp. 143, 144, 145, 152, 153, and 207–8.
Don Fine—pp. 139, 140.
David Gelsanliter—pp. 159–60.
Billy Gillan—pp. 193 and 194.
Herman Gollob—p. 82.
Winston Groom—pp. 217 and 218.
Genta Hawkins—p. 142.
Addie Herder—p. 130.

Joe Luppi—p. 190.

John P. Marquand, Jr.—p. 68.

Peter Matthiessen—pp. 81–82, 214, and 236.

Burroughs Mitchell—pp. 56, 63, 65, 66, 70, 71, 73, 77, 78, and 82–83.

David Morris—pp. 183 and 184.

Muriel Murphy—p. 121.

Stewart Richardson—pp. 161 and 162.

Budd Schulberg—pp. 85, 86, and 87.

Irwin Shaw—pp. 94, 100, 101, 102, 104, 115, 116, and 119.

Wilfrid Sheed—pp. 190 and 191.

Rose Styron—pp. 114, 135, 155, and 250.

William Styron—pp. 69, 70, 109, 110, 118, 128, and 129.

Edmund Trzcinski—pp. 125, 126, and 127.

Miriam Ungerer—p. 189.

Marina Van—p. 187.

Kurt Vonnegut, Jr.—p. 120.

Dick Weber—pp. 218 and 219.

Jack Whitaker—pp. 191 and 192–93.

Clem Wood—pp. 118, 119, 122, 132, 133, 146, 147, and 240.

Bob Wool—p. 148.

❋ ❋ ❋

I'm indebted to the authors and publishers of the following books for the generous use of quotations:

Americans in Paris by Tony Allen, published by Contemporary Books, Incorporated: quoted on pp. 94 and 153–54.

Max Perkins: Editor of Genius by A. Scott Berg, published by E. P. Dutton (Thomas Congdon Books): quoted on pp. 33, 56, 57, 58, 59, 60, and 188.

Montgomery Clift by Patricia Bosworth, published by Harcourt Brace Jovanovich: quoted on pp. 73 and 74.

Paris! Paris! by Irwin Shaw, published by Harcourt Brace Jovanovich: quoted on pp. 96, 101, 115, and 154.

* * *

From James Jones's own books, I found his non-fiction *World War II* indispensable for early autobiographical material quoted on pp. 33, 34, 35, 36, 37, 38, 39, 40–51, 64, 65, 136, 137, 200, and 213–14. I'm grateful to the publisher, Grosset & Dunlap, for permission to draw on this book.

His essay on Marshall, Illinois, quoted on pp. 72 and 74, appeared in the March 1957 issue of *Ford Times*.

I'm grateful to his publisher Delacorte Press for permission to quote from the following:

The Merry Month of May, quoted on pp. 104, 111–12, 113, 123–24, 133, and 153.

Viet Journal, quoted on pp. 32, 34, 36, 37, 147–50, and 151.

Whistle, quoted on pp. 46, 47, 204–5, 237, 238, 239, 240, 254, and 255.

I'm also grateful to his first publisher, Charles Scribner & Sons, for permission to quote from:

Some Came Running, quoted on pp. 78, 79–80, 171, 205, 209, and 228.

The Pistol, quoted on p. 212.

The Thin Red Line, quoted on pp. 105–7.

* * *

I gratefully acknowledge use of the following:

Edna St. Vincent Millay's *Dirge Without Music,*

258

published by Harper & Brothers, quoted in its entirety on p. 16.

William Butler Yeats's *The Lake Isle of Innisfree*, quoted in its entirety on p. 248.

William Faulkner's paragraph from his foreword to *The Faulkner Reader*, published by Random House: quoted on p. 251.

Joan Didion's passages from her article *Gentleman-Ranker* appear on pp. 251 and 252. Her piece was published by *Esquire*, October 1977.

A. B. C. Whipple's article "James Jones and His Angel," which appeared in *Life* magazine, May 7, 1951, was of much help to me on Lowney Handy and the writer's colony. Whipple's piece is quoted on pp. 52–55, of this book.

Budd Schulberg's recollections appeared in *Newsday*, May 15, 1977, and are quoted on pp. 86 and 87.

Irwin Shaw's remarks on pp. 100 and 101 appeared in an interview by Gaby Rodgers in *Newsday*, February 26, 1978.

James Jones's observations on war, quoted on p. 213, are from a speech he gave not long before he died.